TRANSIT

Other Ford-related books by this author include:

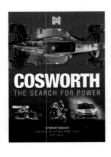 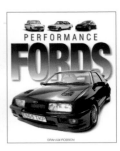 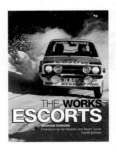 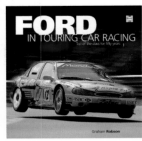

TRANSIT

The 40-year story of Britain's best-loved van

Graham Robson

Foreword by Sir Henry Cooper OBE

FORD

FORD TRANSIT

Haynes Publishing

First published in October 2004

A catalogue record for this book is available from the British Library

ISBN 1 84425 104 7

Library of Congress control no. 2004106164

Published by Haynes Publishing, Sparkford, Yeovil, Somerset, BA22 7JJ, UK
Tel: 01963 442030 Fax: 01963 440001
Int. tel: +44 1963 442030 Int. fax: +44 1963 440001
E-mail: sales@haynes.co.uk
Website: www.haynes.co.uk

Haynes North America, Inc.,
861 Lawrence Drive, Newbury Park,
California 91320, USA

Page-build by G&M Designs Limited,
Raunds, Northamptonshire
Printed and bound in England by
J. H. Haynes & Co. Ltd, Sparkford

Contents

Foreword
by Sir Henry Cooper OBE
Heavyweight boxing champion

My first car was a Ford. My twin brother George and I bought this when we turned professional in 1954. It hadn't been earnings from boxing that paid for it though, because there weren't many of those in the early days – we were both still working as plasterers to make ends meet. It certainly wasn't the best machine I ever owned but it was reliable enough in its way, until it had a horrible accident. It was the sit-up-and-beg model, the Prefect.

As my boxing career developed and I got acquainted with other vehicles, from Alfa Romeo to Rolls-Royce, it never really occurred to me that I would ever run a van, so when I was approached to go into a greengrocery business by my namesake, a man called Harry Cooper, the transportation for this enterprise was probably the last thing on my mind.

To see 'Henry Cooper of Wembley' emblazoned on the side of this thing was a bit of a surprise. Of course it was partner Harry's name as well (or so he said), so I wasn't going to complain, but looking back I suppose it was all a bit of an ambush.

I recall the smell of our Transit rather than anything else, that earthiness which you used to get in old-fashioned grocery shops – certainly not unpleasant, but I will always connect the two somehow.

Of course, another association I have with the Transit is that the Variety Club of Great Britain uses them, and for the same reason that we did – unlike other motor vehicles I've owned, you can take for granted that it will do the job. Never mind carting spuds around, the Sunshine coaches really do carry a precious cargo.

So, the Transit – reasonable to buy, cheap to run, and incredibly dependable.

World-famous boxer Henry Cooper also had a day job in the 1960s – selling greengroceries. The 30cwt Transit flatbed was ideal for collections and deliveries.

Acknowledgements

Without a great deal of help from Ford's enthusiastic Transit team, the Public Affairs staff who back them, and of course the amazing Ford Photographic Department, I would certainly not have been able to write a complete book.

In particular, these people helped me enormously, and I owe a lot to them:

Gordon Bird, Anne-Marie Chatterton, Linda Craddock, Richard Folkson, Barry Gale, Mike Hallsworth, Rod Hammonds, Jim Fowler, Gibb Grace, Dave Grandinett, Dave Hill, Eric Hoile, Don Hume, Angus Macleod, Trevor Mills, Ernur Mutlu, Peter Nevitt, John Packwood, Richard Parry-Jones, Vernon Preston, Barry Reynolds, Alan Selman, Graham Symonds, Gary Whittam and Paul Wilson.

Martin Holmes provided the picture of Mick Jones racing a Transit in Portugal, while Dick Compton, Jim Fowler and Dave Hill provided vital help in locating illustrations. My grateful thanks to them all.

Graham Robson,
Bridport,
Autumn 2004

Introduction

Ford's legendary Transit has become an icon. Famous since the mid-1960s, it sells more strongly with every passing year and the story gets ever more complicated, as sales carry on rising, while more and more varieties keep on appearing.

Maybe this explains why no-one has previously attempted to write the story of the Transit.

Sales figures tell their own story. By the time Ford's famous Transit reaches its 40th anniversary in 2005, it will have outsold –

and outlived – almost every other famous Ford vehicle. Even when I started writing this book, more than five million Transits of one shape or another had already been produced, and the tide was still coming in. More than a quarter-of-a-million Transit-badged machines are being produced every year.

Even so, let's forget the numbers, and the balance sheet. Instead, I want to concentrate on the Transit as a phenomenon. Now, as in earlier years, it is part of Europe's motoring fabric.

Mail deliveries? Courier transport? Hotel courtesy buses? Telecommunications machinery? Plumbers' vans? Motor caravans? Backbone of the utilities? Pop group transportation? Celebrity wheels? Publicity back-up load-carriers? Special-bodied miracles? Builders' lorries? Milk delivery trucks? Recovery vans? Yes, all of those. Think of a job and the Transit probably does it – magnificently.

In short, since 1965, the Transit has meant more, to more people, than any other van-based machine I know. More than that – and Ford is delighted to boast about it – 'Transit' has now entered the English language as a generic brand all of its own. Like 'Hoover', 'Coca Cola', 'Mini, 'Biro' and others, 'Transit' now defines a certain type of vehicle. No matter how hard the opposition tries to change this, their vehicles have been given the same description – and Ford is happy to know that.

Forty years ago, however, Ford's ambitions were modest. Even before Ford-of-Europe was founded, two European companies got together to create 'the common van'. 'Redcap', as it was coded at first, started the never-ending success story which we all see on our roads to this day.

Today's Transit story may be a romance, but there was nothing romantic about the way that it evolved. As one of my Ford contacts explained: 'It's all about how much you can get in the back. People buy payload. Whatever we did, it was never by accident. We always tried to get more into the back …'

And that sums up the worth of this amazingly versatile vehicle. As long as it weighs less than 2 tonnes and will fit inside the capacious platform of a Transit, then the job can be done. Not only that, but it has always been done with style, and with a great deal of flair.

So here is my story of Transit – the First Forty Years – and may I please steal one of the very best advertising slogans of all? 'Job Done.'

Five generations of Transit show just how far the pedigree advanced in 40 years. Left to right: the original van of 1965 (complete with 'diesel nose'), the facelift model which followed in 1978, the original VE6 of 1986, the smiley-face VE83 of 1994, and the all-new-for-2000 model with its choice of front-wheel-drive or rear-wheel-drive.

1 **Where** it all started

Can you even remember a time when there were no Transits? When the choice of medium-sized vans and pick-ups was strictly limited? When you could be sure that a traffic jam was usually headed by an overloaded van? When diesel engines were noisy, smelly and dirty? When delivery vans were slow and ponderous? When no self-respecting private-car owner was ever overtaken by a 'white van man' in a hurry? When no-one went into the local pub and boasted of being a 'white van man'? So long ago, in fact, that the phrase 'white van man' had not even been invented?

It really was a long time ago, right? Almost 40 years ago, in fact. The Transit, which arrived in 1965, changed all that, and continues to do so. Right from the start, it was a product which the world of business wanted – and it terrified its opposition; it still does. From Day One, it was a market leader throughout Europe, and before long it seemed that there was a Transit for every occasion.

Vans, pick-ups, crew buses, chassis/cab and chassis/cowl types were always available, but it was the market place, and the builders of special derivatives who eventually made the range so wide. Think of police vans, mobile radio trucks, hoists for electricity supply companies, school buses, mobile libraries, pop group transport, motor caravans, armoured currency transfer machines, dust carts, milk delivery trucks … no, there are far too many derivatives to list.

In those forty years, rivals have all pitched in, to fight the Transit. Their problem, though, was that they were not first, not better, not backed by a supreme dealer and service support network – and they didn't invent the name. What was the point, it seemed, of having a competent competitor, and spending millions on its image, if a customer walked into the competitor's showroom and asked to see the latest

'Transit'! Ford loved that – still does, for that matter – and rivals hate it.

Origins

When the Transit was 'invented', there was still no co-operation between Ford companies in Europe. Instead, there was intense rivalry. In the early 1960s, Ford cars, vans and trucks were built in two countries – England and West Germany – and in export countries the two companies competed with each other for every sale.

Countries including France, Italy, Holland and Belgium all had thriving Ford dealer networks – all of them operating what was once nicknamed the 'two fishing line' marketing approach. A Ford dealer in those countries could sell products from both factories, and make money in the process. Ford of USA knew this – and encouraged it.

By the early 1960s, however, one important personality – Henry Ford II no less – began to find it irritating. Parachuted into the hot seat at the end of the Second World War, to sort out the mess his senile grandfather had inflicted on the company, by this time HFII had become a formidably successful businessman. To quote his biographer and long-time Ford confidant, Walter Hayes: 'For nearly twenty years, Henry had worried about Ford-of-Europe … with the way it managed and exploited its growing resources. From 1962 his impatience with the way things were, became increasingly evident …'

Although it would be many years before he found time to set up the Ford-of-Europe organisation, he decided to impose his will in every possible way. When Ford-UK and Ford-of-Germany separately decided to develop new medium-size commercial vehicles, HFII put his foot down. Ford-UK already had a new project, coded Thames 800E, in its forward plan, while Ford-of-Germany wanted to replace the Taunus Type FK (Ford Koln) van, which was not a great success.

Even though the new product might be manufactured on two or even more sites, Henry Ford would authorise only one layout. In some ways the German company benefited more than the British concern, for Ford-of-Germany still lacked body-building facilities. A new joint project would make it worthwhile to develop new pressings and assembly facilities, for what the statisticians always called 'The Numbers', made more sense. At that stage, it was meant to have a life, in production, of only eight years, but as we now know, its original style, with only one makeover, would eventually last for 21 years. No wonder it was profitable, and no wonder everyone at Ford now seems to love the Transit so much.

This, then, was the start of what Ford legend now remembers as the 'Common Van'. In the beginning, though, it was more formally coded 'Project Redcap' and was born in 1961, with American specialist, Ed Baumgartner, as the original product planning catalyst. The result was the first ever Ford joint project to be tackled in Europe. Even so, Ford-UK always held design and engineering leadership for the Transit, and carried out almost all of the work, which they did until V184/V185 work began in the mid-1990s.

Even though there were jealousies to be ignored, and inter-company friction to be smoothed away, the planning process eventually worked out surprisingly well. Baumgartner was proud of what had been achieved, but he once commented that as a challenge it must have been easier to put a man on the moon!

For a time, the German engineers, who operated in a rigid, heirarchical manner,

Almost from the day that it was launched, the new Transit became familiar throughout Europe.

What's
in a
name?

The Transit has been so successful that it now defines its own market with customers referring to nearly all commercial vehicles of this size and type as 'Transits' – which makes Ford very happy, but which infuriates their rivals.

According to dictionaries, by the way, Transit is defined as: 'The act or process of going, conveying, or being conveyed, especially over a distance' – and Ford is happy to settle for that.

This particular example of the medium-size Taunus van/mini-bus range was seen outside the Excelsior-Ernst hotel in Cologne.

simply would not relate to the more flexible British approach – and at times when British testing showed up a problem with German components, there was a refusal to admit that a shortcoming existed.

Apart from these personal hitches, engineering work had to embrace good old-fashioned Imperial measure *and* metric measurements. Parts were released separately in the UK and in Germany – with different part numbers – and it was some years before these were rationalised. Between Britain and Germany there was continuous and frantic

travel at all management levels – but the savings mounted up. Later estimates were that $15 million was saved, and the process was on-going.

One major lesson was learnt – which was that there were huge financial benefits to be gained from working together. Confidential reports published after the Transit had gone on sale recommended 'greater standardisation between the two organisations' along with: 'We strongly recommend the establishment of a separate product group comprised of capable

bilingual personnel from both locations to develop and co-ordinate future common programmes ...

'Although substantially greater differences exist between Ford-of-Britain and Ford-of-Germany than exist between the two domestic vehicle divisions, we are convinced these differences are not insurmountable ...'

Nor were they. Two years after the Transit went on sale, Ford-of-Europe would be established, the first two major private car projects being the new Escort (1968) and the Capri (1969).

Before long, 'Project Redcap' soon became known as the 'V-Series' project at Ford-of-Britain, but once it had its proper name – Transit – all other titles were speedily forgotten. Even so, getting as far as that name took time: for ages it was a machine known as the 'V-Class' which looked set to survive to the market place. But 'V' for – what? No-one now seems to remember, for 'V' could have meant 'van', or 'V' could have referred to the vee-layout engines – Vernon Preston, who was the Transit's chassis design engineer, once claimed that it was named after his initial!

In the end, it was apparently Ford-of-Britain's Chairman, Bill Batty, who swept the unromantic 'V' title aside. Not long before assembly was meant to begin, Batty

apparently saw a pilot-build left-hand-drive van to which his German colleagues had fixed a 'Transit' badge, seized upon that, and applied it to the new product.

'Transit', in fact, was not a new name for a Ford – it was already a model name being used on some German-made Taunus vans – but up to this stage it had not yet developed a momentum of its own. All that was about to change.

In 1961, the brief from the top – the top, make no mistake, being on the other side of the Atlantic, in Dearborn, USA – was for the 'Common Van' to replace two existing products – the British Thames 400E, and the German Taunus Transit. Both were successful, both were well-established, and both did similar jobs in the native companies. Not only that, but both were essentially domestic successes, rather than stars in the export market.

By that time, both were technically out of date (old-style petrol engines featured in both ranges, and as yet there was no Ford-built diesel alternative) and both were strictly national, as opposed to international, successes. Neither could be described as visually attractive, and neither handled anything like as well as a private car.

Britain's Thames 400E van, in fact, told its own story. Although it looked smart

Before the Transit came along, Ford's best-selling medium-sized van was the Thames 400E.

The German Taunus Transit was a real ugly duckling of a machine. Along with the British Thames 400E, it was to be replaced by the Transit project.

enough, with a touch of transatlantic influence on the nose, and had independent front suspension, it was a forward-control machine which handled like a sailing boat in a Force Nine wind. Introduced in 1957, it had a 1.7-litre Ford Consul engine, a 1.6-litre Perkins diesel engine option, and until 1964, only had a three-speed gearbox.

By the early 1960s it was out-of-date, and the market place knew it. It was revolution time.

Bare bones

Although both Ford national companies would soon become involved, much of the original 'Project Redcap' work was carried out in Essex by Ford-of-Britain. Product Development – 'engineering' to you and I – was concentrated at Aveley (sometimes known as South Ockendon), in a factory once devoted to building Canterbury motorcycle sidecars. Styling work, in fact, the modification of a package provided by Ford-USA, was finalised in what had originally been a Briggs Motor Bodies facility at Dagenham.

At this time the project was directed by Charlie Baldwin. Fred Ray was Chief Engineer, and his Transit manager was Vernon Preston. Chassis design was led by Fred Ray while body design was Don Ward's responsibility. Preston, who had been working for Ford since 1942, moved over from passenger car to truck engineering work in the 1950s, and had a great deal of experience before this project even began,

including studying the art of 'packaging design' in Dearborn, with Ford-USA.

One-time Standard apprentice Alan Selman, joined Ford in 1959 as Supervisor, Chassis Design, and took up the same title when Transit work began in 1963. Along with Vernon Preston, Alan remembers just how small the Transit engineering team actually was – there were no more than 17 engineers working on the chassis and suspension layout of this all-new product, a total of 24 people including development staff.

Right from the start, Ford wanted to make a major leap forward. Previous vans had often been designed around their payload capacity, at the expense of any technical elegance or roadworthiness. Alan recalls just how awful the handling and the mechanical integrity of the old Thames 400E had been, but with 'Redcap', that was all about to change. Engines would be up front, instead of alongside the driver, or under the seat. This not only made components easy to reach for maintenance, but it would also be much safer: the driver's feet would no longer be the first internal objects to hit the wall in an accident. The accent, too, was to be on rugged simplicity.

There was never, apparently, any intention of keeping independent front suspension, the reputation of which had been destroyed by the Thames 400E on which it had been based on Consul/Zephyr components and had not been durable. At certain speeds it had eventually led to uncontrollable wheel shimmy.

'That was *not* going to happen on the Transit,' Preston recalls, 'I was determined about that.'

Even before true prototypes could be built, the team produced a long-wheelbase 'mule' – which was actually based on a Bedford CA van of the period. This, if nothing else, was a perfect disguise. Engineer Gordon Bird recalls: 'In about 1962, we carved it about to have a front beam axle instead of the Bedford's coil spring independent set-up, and also cut it in half and lengthened it by 16 inches to get the 118in wheelbase we needed. That vehicle then did all the braking and suspension work – all through the programme.

'Then we built two more prototypes based on the old Thames 400E.'

The original layout was completed by an American engineer, Chris Cope, who based the original package on the semi-forward-control Ford-USA Econoline panel van. One advance was that Ford chose to use 14in wheels and tyres – a size that was barely known in Europe, and for which heavy-duty commercial tyres were not then available.

To quote Gordon Bird, who was the original Transit Development Supervisor: 'What made the Transit really stand head and shoulders above its rivals was the fact that here, at least, was a commercial vehicle that was good to drive. Other vans had all sorts of horrible vices, particularly when they were unladen, and were very basic in most respects. But the Transit had handling and roadholding qualities just as good as many cars being built in the mid-1960s.'

Although this was one of those very rare occasions when a new product could be engineered from scratch – there was to be no carryover of existing components, panels or suspension components, and even the engines would be totally new – not everyone could agree on the format of the new model. The fact that the engines were to be mounted up-front ahead of the seating compartment meant that 'Redcap' would either have to be a lot longer than the models it replaced, or that the load capacity would suffer. Therefore, if the load capacity was not to suffer, then the new model would have to be wider than its predecessors.

At Ford, the engineering project codes were LCX and LCY (LC standing for light commercial), with X and Y referring to different wheelbase lengths. Everyone agreed that there *should* be two wheelbase lengths – 106in (2,690mm) and 118in (3,000mm) were chosen, the longer-wheelbase/high-payload types having twin rear wheels – although at one time there were thoughts of providing an ultra-long 'LCZ' model. At the project stage there were huge arguments about the length, the front overhang, and the width. Many objections came from the 'we haven't made one that wide before …' brigade, who were sure that a larger product would spell commercial suicide, but a bit of simple product sampling proved otherwise, and the project went ahead.

Fortunately there was no hurry to settle the design, as the new 'Common Van' would take the place of the two existing models which were still selling well, and would continue to do so for several years. In Germany, much of the competition came

from VW's Transporter, while in the UK the most successful vans came from BMC, Commer and Vauxhall, who made a smaller van best known for its Dormobile conversions. None of these offered big advantages over the Fords, and the cash tills continued to ring out.

Between 1961 and 1963 therefore, the style and layout was gradually worked up, and the engineering of the new machine continued, although no prototypes were actually built. Experience had convinced the planners that a semi-forward-control layout (with the engine tucked up ahead of the bulkhead, but with a very stubby nose) was desirable, and best for safety and packaging reasons. Sketches turned into three-dimensional clay bucks in the USA, at Dearborn, and by early 1963 the

Although the Transit's predecessor, Ford-UK's Thames 400E van, had been a commercial success, it used an obsolete engine (the 1.7-litre four-cylinder from the Consul) and was a forward-control layout, which Ford no longer favoured.

No-one ever called the interior of a German Taunus van luxurious. For the new Transit, Ford engineers were determined to do a lot better.

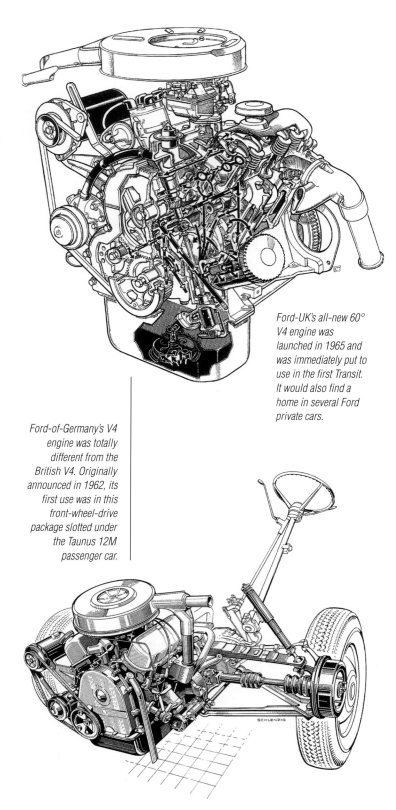

Ford-UK's all-new 60° V4 engine was launched in 1965 and was immediately put to use in the first Transit. It would also find a home in several Ford private cars.

Ford-of-Germany's V4 engine was totally different from the British V4. Originally announced in 1962, its first use was in this front-wheel-drive package slotted under the Taunus 12M passenger car.

finished buck was shipped across the Atlantic to the UK.

Independent to the last, Ford-UK's British styling/design team then made sure that it looked less American and more European (mainly by raising the headlamps, and making the grille more 'truck-like'), and before long it was ready to be turned into real machinery. This was the point at which a payload range of 12cwt to 35cwt (1,344lb/610kg to 3,920lb/1,777kg) was finally chosen.

Although the development 'mules' ran extensively, to build up experience with the chosen mechanical layout, the first definitive prototype did not take to the road until January 1964. After this, of course, the floodgates opened, for in the next 18 months no fewer than 17 hand-built prototypes were put on the roads of Britain and Europe.

In those days, testing equipment was almost non-existent: 'We were still measuring spring deflections,' Bird told me, 'with marker plates and pencils!'

With a style agreed, along with the choice of wheelbases, it was relatively straightforward to set down the bare bones of the structure, for Ford had a great deal of experience in this category. All-steel integral construction was to be specified for the vans, buses and combis; other derivatives including chassis/cab and chassis/windscreen types would look visually similar, but would run on sturdy separate ladder chassis frames, so that the erection of special bodywork and special features was much simplified.

The clever detail which made this possible was the main chassis members which were always present. When the van-type shell was fitted these were welded to the floor pan, but when supplied as a chassis cab, they were boxed in, as expected. Dennis Roberts, the aerospace-trained structures and stress analysis engineer who had done so much to reduce weight in the Cortina project, was mainly responsible for this layout: 'That was the very first time,' today's top engineer Richard Parry-Jones told me, 'that we were able to make a monocoque truck which had closed rail chassis sections, and which could also have a separate frame behind a chassis/cab version.'

One improvement made at this stage was to increase the front wheel track by 1.5in (38mm) although this was not agreed without a struggle. Vernon Preston tells how

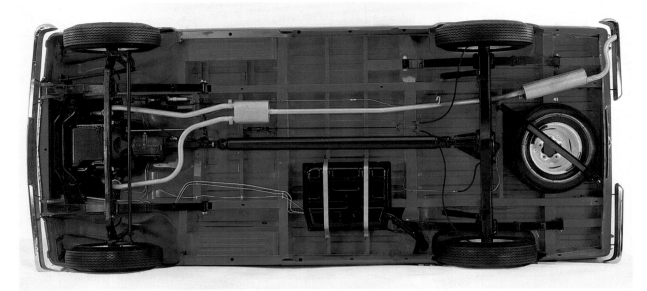

he, with engineering responsibility for the chassis, realised that he could cut the turning circle significantly, but only by first widening the wheel tracks: 'Now, we already had the Product Planning "package book", which specified track dimensions, but I went to see Ed Baumgartner, and asked him for a change. After arguing with him over costs, I got away with it. This gave us a remarkably compact turning circle, far better than our competitors – really, only a London taxi could beat it.'

At this point in their history, Ford saw no advantage in making the new machine technically complex if this would drive up the costs. Nor, at that moment, did they see the need to go for independent front suspension – especially as that used on the Thames 400E seemed to do nothing for the handling! Accordingly, front suspension was by a beam axle with half-elliptic leaf springs, while the beam rear axle would also be supported by half-elliptic leaf springs. Steering was by non-assisted re-circulating ball (a German design), and there was an optional vacuum servo to help add bite to the big drum brakes, this being a real selling point in the commercial vehicle sector.

The big innovation came in the choice of engines. None of the engines currently being used in Taunus Transits in Germany, or in the Thames 400E in the UK, were even considered, for Ford's product planners thought them to be old-fashioned, heavy and inefficient. In any case, Dearborn decreed

that it was time for both companies to invest in a new mid-range engine to take them through the 1960s and 1970s. Much analysis, prompted by heavy hints from Dearborn, went into the study.

One 'given' was the need to save space in the engine bay: this made it almost certain that a vee-formation would eventually be chosen which would be a 'first' for both concerns. Although Ford-of-Germany had never used a six-cylinder engine, in the UK the Zephyrs and Zodiacs used a bulky straight six which was remarkably lengthy. Ford-USA, whose Light Truck expertise was legendary, also made the point, loud and clear, that it didn't really matter how wide a new engine might be, as width was rarely a problem with vehicle engine bays, whereas length often was.

Both teams finally took the hint, and set about developing their own, separate, families of closely related 60° V4 and V6 power units, to be matched by their own in-house transmissions. In each case these engines could be machined and assembled on the same dedicated production lines, and by suitable juggling of bores and strokes, a quite remarkable spread of cubic capacities and power outputs was possible. The new German V4 (coded 'Hummer') was ready in 1962, for use in the front-wheel-drive Taunus 12M, while a V6 derivative followed two years later.

The original British V4 followed in October 1965, when it was launched

Efficient packaging – original Transit style. The short V4 engine lived up front, with the rest of the space being devoted to the driver, passenger and lots of payload. The fuel tank and spare wheel were both placed under the load floor.

simultaneously for the Transit and the new Corsair V4 private car: a V6 engine appeared in the spring of 1966. For the Transit, a gearbox with a side opening for selectors for steering column control was given a new casing, and a direct, centre-floor gearchange. This gearbox was so successful that it would be used until the early 1990s.

Interestingly, Ford eventually offered an automatic transmission option, but very few such installations were ever sold – the marginal loss of operating economy and of performance saw to that. Even so, there would be a few customers who demanded it – and since the same engine/automatic transmission combination had already been engineered for the Corsair and Zephyr/Zodiac range, it was speedily adapted for LCX/LCY.

However, was it really necessary to have not one, but two new families of similar engines? Perhaps we will never know why this happened. At this stage it is enough to report that the British family of engines, coded 'Essex', eventually spanned 1.7 litres to 3.4 litres over a long career, while the German power units ranged from 1.2 litres to 4.0 litres. The British engine was larger and heavier in all its casting details. Both engines could be 'stretched' or 'compressed' quite remarkably. The German engine was so compact that a 1.2-litre was originally manufactured on the tooling in Cologne.

When Ford-of-Europe rationalisation set in with a vengeance, from the late 1970s, the 'Essex' engines were withdrawn although

they lived on in Ford-South-Africa for another decade), while the last of the Cologne-inspired engines was still being made in 2004.

In all that time, too, one or other of these two types were vital building blocks for Ford products. Not only did they provide motive power for Transits, but for Capris, Cortinas and A-Series trucks, Sierras, Zodiacs and Scorpios, and even (in much modified form) in racing Capris and F5000 single-seater racing cars.

Although neither engine was technologically advanced – in any case, on V4 engines, a contra-rotating balance shaft was needed to provide acceptable high-speed balance – they were simple, robust and torquey. Not only that, but they were remarkably compact.

This, in fact, is why the architecture of British V4 engines of 1.7 litres and 2.0 litres were ideal for use in the original British Transit, while German-built 1.5-litre and 1.7-litre V4s were well-suited to the German-inspired versions. Incidentally, because German V4s were installed in German cars like the Taunus 12M, which had six-volt electrical systems, this meant that there were originally two different electrical installations in the Transit. The new 'Common Van'? Not so common, at first ...

The new Transit was a normal-control machine (the engine was ahead of the passenger toe board), but even the 2-litre version of the British 'Essex' V4 was so chunky that it could be accommodated in what was a very short nose. One reason was that the cast-iron cylinder block was, quite literally, wider than it was long – for although it measured only 12.47in (317mm) from front-to-back, it spanned 15.66in (347mm) across (including the cylinder heads). Except that the cylinder heads on the British engine had what was known as a 'Heron' layout (where the combustion chamber recesses were in the top of the pistons, while the heads were totally flat), this was otherwise a thoroughly conventional Ford power unit.

Because the V4 was so much shorter than a conventional four-cylinder in-line power unit, and the engine bay had been profiled to suit, when the time came to package a diesel engine alternative, Ford's designers found themselves in a spot of bother. In those days, although diesel power was still rarely seen in

When Ford came to engineer the diesel-engined Transit, they needed to extend the nose to find space for the Perkins engine. For seven years, therefore, this was known as the 'diesel nose'.

small and medium-sized commercial vehicles, the British company decided that it needed to provide that option in the Transit, although the Germans did not offer a diesel Transit of any type until 1972.

The problem was that neither Ford company was then building its own small compression ignition power unit. This was therefore a big problem. Diesel versions of the new British V4 had already been designed and tested, but only two such engines were built before the project was abandoned. With no other small diesel on the stocks, and with no chance of seeing one developed for some years to come, Ford had to look around for a proprietary unit which might fill the bill. Although several four-cylinder units were available, none of these were of the V4 type.

In the event, the search ended at the Perkins factory in Peterborough, but not without a great deal of expense and soul searching. Ford was already an established customer of Perkins, but these were neither refined, nor powerful, power units. Even though Perkins had a suitably sized unit already on the market – the 1.76-litre Type 4/99 – this was compact, nicely detailed, and already in use as a proprietary conversion in several other cars and trucks. However, it was under-powered and it was a straight four. Worse, it was far too long for the original Transit's bodywork, which had been wrapped closely around the new Ford V4s and their cooling radiators.

One solution would have been to push the Perkins diesel further back in the chassis, but this would have ruined the packaging of the bulkhead, and the foot/pedal spacing.

'We simply couldn't do that,' Preston remembers. 'We had to leave the clutch face in the same place.'

In the end, it was decided to leave the gearbox in its original place (which set the alignment of any cylinder block/bell housing position) and to 'grow' the diesel engine forward into the nose.

Accordingly, the company had to take another brave decision, spend significantly more money on an alternative body style, and provide a protruding nose for the engine bay, which stuck out forward of the unchanged headlamps. For the first few years, all diesel-engined Transits could be identified by that extra-length nose, although it was only the bonnet and front grille which

were different – headlamp pods and front wings remained unchanged.

In many ways the front-end style, complete with its cowled headlamps, its wide-mouth grille (petrol) and jutting chin front end (diesel), looked Transatlantic, for at this stage there is no doubt that Dearborn still exercised much influence on the looks of European Fords. Prototypes looked even more 'American' than the shape finally chosen. Even so, the style was worked on and finalised in Ford's Dagenham-based styling studios, and was at once more distinctive and more practical than the twin products it was to replace.

Although the cab featured a rather 'sit-up-straight' driving position, with pedals

One base model – but two nose styles. The white Transit, with a horizontal grille motif, is as originally styled, and was powered by V4 engines but the red van, with an extended nose and squared-up grille, needed that shape to accept the bulkier Perkins diesel power unit. When V6 engines were fitted (in SVO applications) they too needed the lengthened nose.

sprouting through the floor (pendant pedals would follow later), the general layout was much more car-like than the old Thames 400E had been. With the engine, and therefore its gearbox, in a conventional car-style place, there were no oddities in control positioning either. Behind the cab, however, the requirements of the market place – a cube is a cube, is a cube – meant that the team then concentrated on making it as practical and versatile a load-carrier as possible. There would be two wheelbases – 106in (2,692mm) and 118in (2,997mm) – with a huge variation in possible working payload, which originally spanned 1,345lb (610kg) to 3,930lb (1,782kg).

Even at the outset, Ford intended the range of different models to be colossal. According to the publicists, no fewer than 78 separate models were originally listed (this, of course, including all the body derivatives, different engines, and other major options), and this figure did not need to count in what the specialist industry was already planning.

Even the basic vans could be built with slam rear doors or a tailgate, slam or sliding cab doors, and with or without a side loading door. Then there was the possibility of ordering nine, 12 or 15-seater buses, chassis/cab or chassis/windscreen versions,

and of seeing every possible type of special coachwork fitted afterwards.

As Barry Gale (who became Chief Programme Engineer on the ultra-successful Transit for the 2000s) reminded me: 'Right from the start, the long-wheelbase Transit's cube and its doors were arranged to accept the loading of standard 8ft x 4ft sheets of wood or plasterboard, or whatever on the floor. Even today, when we have all gone metric, as far as builders are concerned, that is still a standard measurement – even in Europe!'

Testing, testing ...

Once the big decisions, and the style, had been settled, the development team swung rapidly into action. By the spring of 1965, no fewer than 20 hand-built prototypes, including the 'mules' had been put together, and were pounding around Ford's Boreham airfield (which was then being used as a development facility, as well as the company's Motorsport centre), as well as on the motorways, mountain passes and by-ways of Europe. Because the 2-litre Transit was a lot more powerful than any of its ancestors – and, indeed, more powerful than any of its rivals (Ford was always proud of that) – a lightly laden prototype could also

All Transits, however special, started from the simple basis of this 'semi-forward control' layout.

New V4 engines

Many years before the Transit went on sale, Ford laid down compact new families of engines, for use in its cars and light/medium commercial vehicles. Although Ford-USA controlled both companies, and laid down general strategy, Ford-of-Britain and Ford-of-Germany were allowed to develop competing ranges. Both concerns designed new overhead-valve 60° V4 and V6 engines, which in each case, were machined and assembled on carefully integrated transfer line equipment.

Over the years, Ford-of-Britain's 'Essex' range spanned 1.7-litre (V4) to 3.1 litre (V6), while the entirely different Ford-of-Germany 'Cologne' engine range spanned 1.2-litre (V4) to 4-litre (V6).

Before advances made under Ford-of-Europe were established, Genk-built Transits used Ford-of-Germany V4s, while British-built Transits used Ford-UK 'Essex' V4s and a few V6s.

Both these families of engines were used in a wide variety of cars and trucks. Such engines were found in private cars as diverse as Capris, Cortinas, Corsairs, Granadas, Sierras and Scorpios, and were manufactured from 1962 until the present day.

be very fast. Night-time motorists caught, and overtaken, by one of those vans were among the first to see the phenomenon of 'white van man', for cruising speeds of 75mph were apparently normal, and top speeds of up to 90mph or even 95mph were certainly possible.

Gordon Bird recalls that: 'Drivers were often stopped by the police in the early days – but only because they wondered how a commercial vehicle could be so quick, and how the project was going on!'

In fairness, an early Transit, fully laden and driven quickly, could also look like a real handful, for at high speeds it was not directionally stable: 'There was too much weight towards the rear,' Alan Selman recalls, 'and at first the tyre technology was lacking. It tended to wander quite a lot – but the best thing was not to fight that with corrections, but to leave the wheel alone!'

Because Ford-of-Germany proposed to use German-type V4 engines in European-built Transits, the British development team made prototypes with German parts.

'We shipped them over there,' Selman told me, 'then carried on testing our own vans. A few months later we thought we had to see how those vans were going on in Germany. So we went over there, and found the vans parked up, as clean as the day we had built them. They hadn't turned a wheel! The Germans didn't think they had to do anything like that – that we had already taken care of it!'

After two years, the British prototypes were well-worn due to the work they had completed, while the German products had virtually not been used at all. Prototypes soon went as far north as Finland to look for the worst of winters, and down to Portugal in summer, where the temperatures were high, and some of the roads were very dusty.

'When the prototypes went to Portugal,' Bird recalls, 'we lost touch with them for ten days! Then I got a phone call from the Spanish/French border, telling me that the team had been impounded.

'The Spanish border guards couldn't understand why a van was carrying a lot of plastic water carriers full of water – we did that to weight them down – was this booze, was it drugs, or what? Our lads had to go to find a local Spanish Ford dealer, to come back to the border, and to explain, before they were released!'

Boreham, as a test track, was useful, but not ideal for high-speed work. British motorways, particularly the M2 motorway in Kent, and West German autobahns (neither of them busy nor overcrowded in those halcyon days) gave every opportunity for prolonged high-speed cruising, much of it carried out at night.

'Everything came together well,' Bird told me, 'though we had a major upheaval halfway through, when for policy reasons, we changed over from Girling to Lockheed brakes. And then there were big noise problems – we always had big noise problems.

In fact, his colleague Richard Folkson later quipped: 'There were two enormous sound booms at about 110dB – just like Concorde taking off! We fixed those!'

While all this was going on, however, Ford was already engaged in another race against time – a race to find somewhere to build the new 'Common Van', and to get it into the showrooms before the end of 1965.

2 Building
on two sites

Right from the start, the question which faced Project Redcap's team was – where should the new model be assembled? Both Ford-UK and Ford-of-Germany wanted to adopt this as 'their' own project, but with most of the engineering work carried out by Ford-of-Britain, getting real co-operation was going to take time, so there was no lack of suggestions.

National pride, naturally, came into the reckoning, but there was also another important factor. As the 1950s ended, both of Ford's principal factories, one in England and the other in West Germany, were already bursting at the seams. In Dagenham, and in Cologne, the original sites which had been set up in the 1920s, were teeming with cars, trucks, vans and tractors – and both companies were looking to expand.

The situation at Ford's British factory was typical. Although the plant had been enlarged mightily since building its first truck in 1931, it was already building thousands of Anglias and Zephyr/Zodiacs every week, and it was also building hordes of tractors, heavy trucks and the still-popular Thames 400E van which 'Redcap' would replace, one day.

For a time Ford-UK, however, thought that it had the situation in hand – but soon had to change its mind. Although a brand-new PTA (paint, trim and assembly) building had recently been commissioned at Dagenham, the development of a new car (to be named Cortina, and later to become a world-wide best seller) meant that this site would eventually only have the capacity to build private cars.

Suddenly, it seems, new factories would have to be found. First of all, Ford-UK decided to build a new car assembly plant at Halewood near Liverpool, where there would also be a massive transmissions plant alongside it. That way, it would be able to move the assembly of mass-market Anglias

and their successors to a new site. At almost the same time Ford-UK also elected to build a factory at Basildon in Essex dedicated to assembling tractors and to extend the lease of an ex-aircraft factory at Langley in Buckinghamshire. The move to Langley in 1960 was to be the salvation of the commercial vehicle division.

Ford-of-Germany, with a little bit more elbow-room, was first of all able to expand the Cologne facility, but it was not long before they had to look further away. Soon they were attracted to two areas in Continental Europe where heavy industry was declining and development grants were available, and where governments were anxious to see Ford set up shop.

One of these was at Genk in Belgium, but just over the border from Germany, while the other was south of Cologne, at Saarlouis, which was itself very close to the border with France.

A multi-million dollar jigsaw

This, though, was only the beginning. Because Henry Ford II in Dearborn controlled all the purse-strings, he had to approve of every major investment in 'his' company. Although he was well-travelled, and certainly knew a lot more about Europe than his underlings (Lee Iacocca, the self-publicist who was on the way to becoming the 'father' of the Mustang was particularly scathing about the European operations, but never stayed over long enough to learn more), he was not about to throw money at new factories without a lot of analysis.

Inexplicably, in fact, it would take him several more years to acknowledge that there was little economic sense in making similar, although not identical, products in two different factories. Even though he had always directed that 'Redcap' was to be a joint project between the British and the Germans, he had still allowed each concern to specify its own range of V4 engines, and for the new vans to be built under different roofs.

All of Ford's planners agreed that the 'light truck' market was immediately large enough to support the manufacture of Transit on two sites – one of them in Great Britain itself, the other in Europe. British Transits, using mainly British running gear (engines, transmissions and the like), would be the only versions produced with right-hand *and* left-hand steering, and would look after the British and traditional Ford-UK export territories. German (or, more strictly, Belgian-built) Transits would use Ford-of-Germany running gear, almost always have left-hand-steering, and cater mainly for the potentially massive European market.

That said, there was still scope for much interchange between nations of body panels and other components. As with its cars, Ford was already dedicated to inter-plant transfers of hardware, as anyone who stood and watched the terminals of the English Channel, or the freight trains of Western Europe, already knew.

There was such an enormous demand for new Cortinas, almost all of which were being assembled at Dagenham, that when the old Thames 400E assembly lines were finally

The original style Transit was produced between 1965 and 1978.

Langley

In Britain, the Transit's first assembly line was set up at Langley, not far from London's Heathrow Airport. Originally built by the Hawker aircraft company in 1938, Langley's first product was the world-famous Hurricane fighter aircraft, which along with the Spitfire, did much to help the RAF win the Battle of Britain in 1940. Langley later built Tempest and Typhoon aircraft, and in post-war years was integrated with other Hawker-Siddeley Group operations.

When it became redundant, Ford took over the plant, converting it to manufacture trucks and other commercial vehicles. Final assembly of Thames 400E vans began in 1960 and these were replaced by the very first Transits, in 1965.

For the next seven years, Transit bodywork was pressed and assembled in Southampton, but final assembly remained at Langley.

In 1972, however, final assembly of the Transit range was centred at Southampton, where it has remained ever since.

Transit assembly at Langley in the late 1960s. Such was the demand that the tracks always seemed to be overcrowded.

The Langley plant, close to London's Heathrow Airport, was the Transit's original British home. Hundreds of Transits were assembled every day (there is less than one day's output, seen here, in the delivery park), and demand was always high. The M4 motorway is at the bottom right of this view.

stripped out in 1960 with the space immediately reallocated and redeveloped to allow more cars to be produced. Similarly, when the old Transit Taunus was killed off in Cologne, its successor would find a home elsewhere.

There was, however, enough space to produce new-generation V4/V6 engines at Dagenham *and* in Cologne. At Dagenham, Ford spent more than £20 million on no less than 44 acres of floor space, for what was certainly the most advanced engine manufacturing facility in Europe at that time. It was a new factory block which would embrace transfer-line machining and the latest types of mechanised assembly aids (although there were no computers in evidence and these would follow in the future). Before long, those engines would be supplied to cars being built at Dagenham, at Halewood – and for the Transit.

In the meantime, the Thames 400E, and eventually the replacement British Transit, had found its first home, at Langley. Immediately to the north and west of London's Heathrow Airport, and close to the M4 motorway at Slough, Hawker (later Hawker-Siddeley) had built thousands of famous Second World War fighter aircraft

In 1965, much of the Transit's body shell was pressed and assembled at this ex-Briggs Motor Bodies plant near Southampton Airport at Eastleigh. The works had been built to assemble and repair Spitfire fighter aircraft in the Second World War and in those days there was space to spare, but by the 2000s, every inch of ground had been developed. This aerial view faces north, with the city of Southampton behind the camera.

Early days, but proud of it. The Langley workforce greets the completion of the 100,000th British-built Transit in 1968.

such as the legendary Hurricane at this factory, but it had now become redundant. Ford took it on, eventually electing to make it the centre of its British commercial vehicle assembly business, and finding space not only to build the large D-Series trucks, but also the 400E and later, the new Transit as well.

Yet this still left them with the search for body shell supplies. By 1963, Dagenham's body plant was already at full stretch (the demand for Cortinas – more than 250,000 every year – saw to that), but fortunately there was an alternative. Briggs Motor Bodies, independent until 1953, but then bought by Ford, had opened up a pressings and component factory at Eastleigh, north of Southampton, in 1949. Here was yet another ex-Second World War fighter aircraft assembly factory (this time it was the equally legendary Spitfire range which had taken shape close to the nearby airfield), which could be expanded, modernised, and put to use for Ford's benefit.

Ford started using the Southampton plant to supply body components and assemblies to Dagenham in 1957, and to Langley from 1960. Light van (Anglia-based) work had followed in 1961, but that facility was transferred to Halewood in 1964 when the Anglia range was relocated to Merseyside.

Here was an opportunity. Southampton, therefore, was re-equipped once again, this time to concentrate on body, paint and trim activities for medium vans and heavy trucks, to support the burgeoning Langley facility. From 1965, therefore, Transit body shells were to be produced at Southampton before being transported the 60 miles of congested south-eastern England to Langley.

Movement of 'building blocks' in and out of the gates of Langley was intense, for this was almost purely an assembly, not a manufacturing, factory. This meant that engines and transmissions would all have to come from Dagenham. In the mid-1960s, remember, that although the new M4 swept past the front gates, the motorway system was incomplete; there was no M3 between London and Southampton, and the M25 was still only a twinkle in some planners' eyes.

Ford-of-Germany had similar problems, and eventually solved them by building a massive new plant at Genk in Belgium. Actually, it was only the traditional layout of

long-established national borders which placed this ex-coal mining region in Belgium at all, for it was in the flat lands to the east of Brussels, where Belgian, Dutch and German territory jostled for space. This land had repeatedly been fought over in the previous century.

Almost exactly mid-way between Brussels and Ford's European plant at Cologne, Genk was also hard by the Albert Canal. As far as Ford and the two governments were concerned, it had two major advantages: there was plenty of space to build a new factory, and a lot of workers close by who were looking for employment.

First opened in 1964, Genk began in a modest way by assembling German Ford

Formula 1 triple World Champion Jackie Stewart, a great believer in road safety, used this Transit when travelling to visit school children in 1973.

Opposite: *Longleat Safari Park in Wiltshire.*

Question: how many people could you get into a new Transit van in 1965? Answer: 48, at Barking College.

cars, but it was an obvious place for the Transit to find a European home, which it duly did from the very launch of this new product. Quickly able to match Langley's assembly rates, and expanding very rapidly indeed, it would also take on the assembly of Cortinas in 1977. From 1982, Genk became the home, not only of Transit in Europe, but of every Sierra, and in the 1990s the centre of Mondeo assembly too. In 2001, more than 100,000 Transits would be produced in a single calendar year.

By that time, Genk was larger than the Cologne plant which had once been its 'parent', was four times as large as Southampton, and was producing seven times as many vehicles as the Hampshire facility.

Launch

While all this factory building and conversion was going ahead, the Transit project was hurtling towards what is known as 'Job One' in the motor industry – the point at which the first production vehicles roll off the assembly line. To allow the delivery pipe-line to fill up, 'Job One' is often

months ahead of the date at which the new machine meets its public. As the Transit was due to be launched in October 1965, it meant that the first new vans needed to be built during the summer.

'We met our engineering schedule, right through the programme,' Vernon Preston says, 'which was a great surprise to the engineering people. In the past they'd been used to our timing slipping …'

At Langley, in fact, it was all-change time, for Ford had chosen to introduce not one, but two new models, in the same year. First of all the large range of trucks, the Thames Traders, had to give way to the D-Series models, which would become best sellers, but the Transit would soon follow them.

The atmosphere at Langley in the summer of 1965, therefore, can be imagined. With two old models to be swept away and two new ranges to fill up the ex-aircraft assembly buildings instead, there was a maelstrom of breaking down, clearing out, and building up of new facilities. At such times, the existence of the motor industry's summer holidays – a time quite wrongly called 'Shut Down' – can be invaluable, for it was at that time that the Transit facilities were finally put in place.

The very first of Ford's new range of vans actually came off the line at Langley on Monday, 9 August 1965, the trickle soon turned into a stream, and the stream into a torrent. It wasn't long before Transits filled every possible parking place, out of sight, both at Ford premises and at Ford dealerships. Alan Worters, Ford of Britain's chief engineer in charge of power units, unveiled the new V4 engines to the media on 1 October, and within a week the public learned of the existence of the new products which used them – the Corsair private car, and the Transit.

Straight away, it was clear that this was not just a replacement for the Thames 400E (British) and Taunus Transit (German) vans, but a new type of product altogether. Compared with the products it replaced, it was larger, faster, more versatile – and was clearly the beginning of a very long and successful life. With short or long wheelbases, low or high roofs, single or twin rear wheels, and a whole range of possible payloads, it almost sold itself. In marketing-speak, it offered 'a lot of "cube" for the money …'

Ford surprised everyone from the very

Some people will do anything to get their names in the paper. Stunt-man Steve Matthews jumped 15 cars in 1985 to raise money for a cancer charity.

Pepsi's use of a gigantic drinks can, behind the Transit chassis/cab, was typical of the way that clients customised the earlier machines.

outset, by selling the Transit at remarkably low prices. At launch in October 1965, the short-wheelbase, petrol van, with a 610kg payload, retailed for only £542, and of course there was no purchase tax (the predecessor to VAT) to be paid on that. For comparison, at this time the tax-paid price of Ford's cheapest car, the Anglia 105E, was £492, and the Anglia De Luxe was priced at £552.

At the same time, the publicists trumpeted the real advances that had been made on the new van – such as the use of a printed-circuit instrument panel, an optional steering column lock, an alternator as standard equipment on the engine, safety belt attachment points, and 5,000-mile (8,000km) service intervals. It wasn't long before tubeless tyres and halogen headlamps were also added to the specification.

It's no exaggeration to say that once launched, and once available for inspection, that Transit sales took off like a rocket; far in advance of what the sales force had ever forecast. Ford's competitors, we now know, were shocked by the new Transit, so much so that they all scurried back to their drawing boards to see how their secret new projects could be improved. Vauxhall-Bedford was apparently so depressed that it cancelled a brand-new van, and started all over again.

When it came to gaining exposure, Ford knew its stuff, so it made sure that early examples of the chassis/windscreen derivatives, complete with the sturdy ladder chassis frame, went off to the motor caravan makers before the Transit was officially launched. Only one week *after* launch, Martin Walter (using their famous 'Dormobile' trade mark), Coachwork Conversions and Canterbury Industrial Products all had Transit motor caravans on display at the Earls Court Motor Show.

The Transit was ideally packaged for conversion into a motor caravan. Soon after launch in 1965, it had established market leadership in that sector.

It was only when private car testers got their hands on the Transit motor caravan conversions that the world suddenly learned just how much better this machine was than its predecessors. Writing about a Coachwork Conversions' 'Freedom' four-berth caravan, in *Autocar* in March 1966 – a machine which was based on a short-wheelbase van with the 1.7-litre V4 engine – Stuart Bladon had this to say: 'Although the engine is at the extreme front of the vehicle, the forward overhang is no more than in the average small car, and yet there is scarcely any intrusion of the engine compartment rearwards into the cab …

'From the driving seat both of the abbreviated front-wing peaks are in view, with the fall-away bonnet, but allowance has to be made for the prominent wrap-round of the front bumper in confined manoeuvring.

'The front seats are lower than before, and the whole arrangement of driving position, with well-raked wheel, and the rather shallower windscreen, now give the Transit much more similarity to an ordinary car than to a van from the cab.

'A four-speed gearbox with sturdy floor-mounted change replaces the previous model's three-speed column-change unit … The gear change is a little notchy and heavy

– almost lorry-like in its action. The gear lever mounting is intentionally rather far forward, so that access across the cab or to the main body of the van from the front is not obstructed …

'As on Ford cars, the Transit steering is very light … The low effort needed at parking speeds, and the exceptionally good lock, make it an easy vehicle to handle in confined quarters.

'When the details of the Transit were first announced, it came as a surprise to learn that Ford had gone back to live axles on half-elliptic leaf springs, after having independent front suspension on the predecessor, but the proof of what might have seemed a retrograde move is certainly to be found in the vehicle's extremely good behaviour on the road …'

I have quoted major extracts from this original test because they show just how surprised the pundits actually were by the new Transit. Hard-nosed commercial vehicle operators, of course, were even more impressed by the 'Bottom Line' figures, but as far as they *and* the drivers were concerned, this was a big advance on the old Thames 400E/Taunus Transit models.

In the winter of 1965/66, the Transit's reputation spread rapidly, orders went through the roof, and Ford found itself with newly established assembly lines which were already full. Waiting lists built up – which was at once gratifying and frustrating, especially for the customers. Fleets did their sums – slide rules in those days, not computers or calculators, don't forget – and it wasn't long before we started to see prestige brand names – oil companies, public utilities and the main motorists' back-up services (AA and RAC) – painted on to the side of these amazing machines.

Sales surged ahead. In Great Britain, no fewer than 18,111 Langley-built Transits were registered before the end of 1965; 22,667 would follow in 1966, and 25,518 in 1967. To a layman, maybe those figures mean little. Let me, therefore, point out that before long, one-in-three of all such medium-sized vans sold in the UK were Transits, and that this would edge up to 40 per cent by the mid-1970s. Within three years, the Transit, like the Hoover vacuum cleaner and the Biro ball-point pen, had imprinted its brand name on the public for a complete class of industrial product …

One reason, for sure, was that the Transit seemed to offer more – a lot more, in terms of payload, capacity, versatility and sheer capability – than its immediate rivals. As far as Ford dealers were concerned, too, it was so much better, in every way, than the old

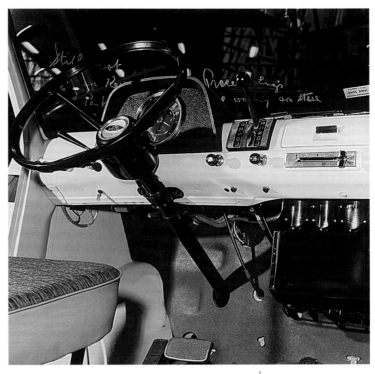

Thames 400E range that the salesmen were positively enthused!

Word about the Transit spread very rapidly, and it wasn't long before the new model was being put to some uses which Ford had never envisaged. It was one thing

This candid camera shot not only shows the simple instrument layout of the original Transit, but the position of the optional automatic transmission gear change lever.

Most early-model Transits were V4 powered, with this horizontal-motif grille style. Castrol, one of Britain's major oil companies, soon added Transits to its fleet.

Suitably equipped original-spec Transits were ideal for use as milk delivery vehicles.

Ah yes, the good old days of the late 1960s, when businesses still provided the personal deliveries for such staples as bread.

for a Transit to be used for home delivery of milk and groceries, and Ford even got used to the idea of hard-working Transits being 'doubled-shifted' (some would be on the road for up to 20 hours a day) – but could they ever have forecast that French

undertakers would discover, to their joy, that a Transit van would accept two standard-sized coffins, side-by-side, between the wheelarches?

Since the Transit was soon taken up by the AA, the RAC, the police and many

Transit

ambulance services, any further promotion by Ford itself was superfluous. If a potential customer needed to know what a new Transit might do for him, all he had to do was to stand outside in the high street, and watch the traffic as it went past him.

Apart from the emergency services, of course, gas, electricity and water supply utilities also began to build up their fleets, so one could soon see a gaily coloured Transit close to a hole in the road, under a lamp post which was being maintained, or near any urban floods which might break out.

After a night at the pub, how about fish and chips from a mobile 'chippy'? Why not? Transits were soon doing that job; an ice cream on a warm day? The same solution. Delivery of TVs, household goods, furniture and anything for the new house? A Transit would invariably do the honours. What about carrying children on the school run, or on educational and sporting trips? You've guessed it – there was a Transit for all such occasions.

Pop groups, of course, soon discovered the Transit, although in some cases they had to wait until they could afford run-down, battered, old examples. In this musical scene, there was a mysterious, but totally logical, social and musical hierarchy.

Bands just getting established tended to store their kit in a scruffy old van, drive half the night between gigs, then maybe roll out their sleeping bags on the load floor to save on expenses. Established groups bought new Transits to carry their mass of gear, and travelled separately. Superstar groups tended to have bigger, more specially equipped Transits, and used their 'roadies' to do all the hard work.

Theme and variations

To get the show on the road, Ford concentrated on its basic range – short and longer wheelbases, three engines, and several different body types – but it wasn't long

How many elephants can you get into a Transit van? Even if they are young ones, only two! London Regents Park Zoo in 1965.

The obvious way to carry a 49ft long dinosaur model, from Kent to a new natural history park in Scotland, was by Transit.

Legendary boxing champion Mohammed Ali hands over a Transit ambulance/bus to the Variety Club of Great Britain.

before the continued efforts of the development engineers began to kick in.

Within a year, the under-powered Perkins 4/99 diesel engine was replaced by the more powerful 4/108 variety, although even this 49bhp oil-burner was not really up to the job, and not competitive with the petrol engines already being specified. Ford knew this, but had no immediate alternative and it was not until 1972 that a permanent cure was available.

From mid-1967, Ford sprung a major

In the early days, Transits were used for almost every purpose. Here was a Swiss project, using Transits for railway maintenance.

surprise. Was there really any demand for automatic transmission on a Transit? Maybe not on hard-working vans, but perhaps, in limited quantities, in Transits which were laid out as buses, where some degree of sophistication might sell. Whatever, three-speed Borg Warner automatic transmission (as already mated to V4 engines in the Corsair and the Zephyr) became optional, and would then stay in the price lists.

For the next two or three years, the accent was then on making the interior more

The Transit was, and still is, totally classless – which explains why it felt so right to use a minibus to arrive at Glyndebourne in the late 1960s.

The famous British pop group, Brian Poole and the Tremeloes, used this early-model petrol-powered Transit mini-bus in 1966.

'Homepride' flour buyers helped finance the purchase of this Transit bus for a children's home in 1970.

No fewer than 200 one-time rickshaw drivers traded up to using Transit buses on Hong Kong island in 1970 – ideal transport for crowded city streets.

'liveable'. What Ford called a new 'safety' fascia appeared in 1968 (along with a parcel shelf for the first time), and at the end of 1970, car-type face-level ventilation was added to that general arrangement.

Even at that stage, Ford's Special Vehicle Option department (SVO) had begun to work on the myriad non-standard versions of the Transit which the customers demanded. Until the mid-1980s, SVO was based at the Langley plant, rather than in the design/engineering buildings in Essex. In many cases it was quite impractical to

engineer the changes and special fittings inside Ford, so a network of suppliers, consultants and special purpose companies was soon built up.

The SVO department should not be confused with SVE (Special Vehicle Engineering), the latter being the team which did the design and development work required to turn good ideas into practical components and fitments. Although SVE was, and still is, an exciting-sounding technical area which tends to spend much time working on high-performance private

福特十四座位巴士 FORD TRANSIT 14 PASSENGER LIGHT BUS

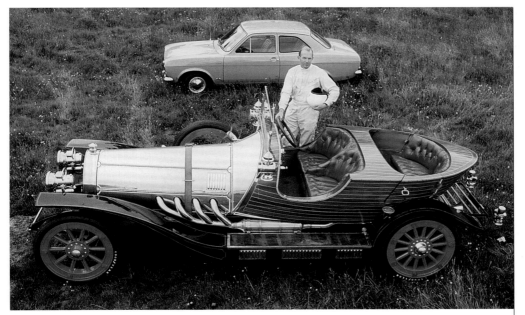

cars, it was also very active in the Transit operation.

SVO and its products have usually been immensely profitable, and spread so far that, before long, up to 40 per cent of all Transits would have SVO content in one form or another. Their work should never be confused with other, conventional, strategies which produce RPOs – or regular production options.

So, what is the difference between an RPO and an SVO? An RPO, by definition, includes the word 'Regular', which means

that a feature – which may be anything from automatic transmission or air conditioning – is listed in catalogues, generally available, and taken up by any general customer. A perfect example of this would be anti-lock brakes, once a formidably costly option, but now available to one and all.

On the other hand, Special Vehicle Options tend to be more specific, and more useful to one particular fleet customer. This could be anything from the way that a van body was specified, to the way that extra

wiring and electrical equipment was
integrated.

As Angus MacLeod, a supervisor in SVE,
once told me: 'Fleet requests are very
important to us. There are many fleet
customers who come to us, saying: "We
would really like to buy the Transit, but …"
– and it is that "but" which usually sees us
springing into action.

'Of course we could let that customer go
off to a specialist to have the job done, but
we might just lose the sales, which would
never do. In any case, if we, Ford, do the
job, we retain the warranty …'

*This was what Transit
engineering was all
about – for use as a
hard-working delivery
vehicle. Beer and a
pasty, anyone?*

*The original 'York' diesel
engine of 1972 was a
sturdy unit, with much
development locked
inside – and a great
advance over the Perkins
unit which it replaced.*

wiring and electrical equipment was
integrated.

As Angus MacLeod, a supervisor in SVE,
once told me: 'Fleet requests are very
important to us. There are many fleet
customers who come to us, saying: "We
would really like to buy the Transit, but …"
– and it is that "but" which usually sees us
springing into action.

'Of course we could let that customer go
off to a specialist to have the job done, but
we might just lose the sales, which would
never do. In any case, if we, Ford, do the
job, we retain the warranty …'

A Special Vehicle Option could – and still
can – be almost anything:

'We cover tyres to roof racks, front
bumper to back bumper. British Telecom, by
the way, is Ford's biggest single customer,
world-wide …'

To any Transit watcher, it is fascinating to
note that items originally specially developed
for one purpose (an SVO) can become a
regular production option, and finally could
even become standard equipment on all
Transits. Over the years the SVE/SVO people
developed so many desirable fittings that
they were rarely stumped by a request.

'Once an SVO option was engineered, it
immediately went "into our back pockets",
and was available to the next customer who
came along. That can cover something
extremely simple, like a bit of wiring, to the
virtual re-engineering of the entire vehicle …

'SVO can tackle projects for which very
few vehicles are ever likely to be built, and
we are so flexible that we can also contact,
and co-operate with, outside suppliers for
one particular job. But it is a continuous
source of amusement to all of us, as to what
a particular customer may want. It isn't
always glamorous, providing for these
customers, but there is always a lot of
surprise and delight!'

When the market had settled down, and
knowledge of the SVO business had spread
far and wide, up to one in three of all

Transits being built have had some sort of SVO content in their specification. Interestingly enough, the Genk plant has habitually processed more SVO Transits than the Southampton plant – one being that the European mainland market (Germany and Holland in particular) seemed to be more SVO minded.

So, do the assembly plants love SVO items, or hate them?

'Well,' Angus grinned, 'they hate us, sometimes, I guess. What the plants would

Penthouse magazine sponsored a team of racing Escorts in 1975, and naturally chose Transits for support vehicles.

For many years, Ford Motorsport used V6-engined Transits as support vehicles. Just for fun, in 1979, the organisers of the Rally of Portugal organised a pre-event slalom test – for service vehicles. Ace mechanic Mick Jones drove this machine in the test, but the result is not known. (Martin Holmes)

love to do, best of all, is build nothing else but white, low-roof, short-wheelbase vans all the time – so in some ways we are a nuisance to them. But, seriously, I think the plants realise that SVO has become a major part of

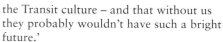

the Transit culture – and that without us they probably wouldn't have such a bright future.'

Even by the early 1970s Ford had developed an 'ambulance package' which, among other things, included an 'Essex' V6 petrol engine. Although this was directly and closely related to the standard V4 petrol engine around which the Transit had been engineered, the V6 was much bulkier – longer and heavier – and was definitely a tight squeeze.

Until 1986, and the arrival of the VE6, this V6 engine could be fitted, with difficulty, behind the 'diesel nose', but once the VE6 came along (see Chapter 4) the new 'fast front' style was shaped to suit it. Ambulances fitted with the V6 were much faster, of course, but – most importantly – they were also smoother and more effortless.

Although many such V6 conversions would be carried out, this engine never became an RPO. Motorsport teams such as Ford's own 'works' operation at Boreham, and many other private owners, found the V6 conversion to be ideal for their use in service 'chase' vans. A few of them even indulged in tuning up the V6 engine itself. When such a personally modified Transit enjoys more than 150bhp, the performance potential may be realised!

In 1971, it was time for another phase of technical up-grades to appear, when Ford introduced single-leaf elliptic springs instead of the original multi-leaf variety, and by 1973 radial ply tyres and servo-assisted front-wheel disc brakes had both been standardised. Both were a real advance, and both were 'firsts' for vans in this market sector.

The bad news for Ford – and perhaps I will never be forgiven for mentioning this – is that the Transit soon became famous for operating on the wrong side of the law, as well as the right side. Ford hates the view that the Transit is a great machine for the underworld to use – but the facts bear it out.

London's Metropolitan police were quoted as saying that the Transit had become 'Britain's most wanted van', and that: 'Ford Transits are used in 95 per cent of bank raids. With the performance of a car, and space for 1.75 tons of loot, the Transit is proving to be the perfect getaway vehicle.'

By the early 1970s, in fact, the Transit had built up a momentum of its own in all walks of life, which made it Britain's best-selling commercial vehicle, a title which it has never relinquished since then. Customers all over the world, it seems, were clamouring for Transits, but Ford often met trade and political difficulties in satisfying that demand.

The solution, in many cases, was to use the motor industry's magic acronym – CKD – to help set-up local assembly plants. CKD means 'completely knocked down', which is industry-speak for the supply of kits of parts to far-flung locations, where a local labour force can weld, hammer, bolt and screw them together.

Starting from premises in Istanbul, Ford-Otosan of Turkey was first to get in on this act, in 1967, and by 1970 they were assembling 1,100 Transits a year. Then, in 1971, there was a real surge, when Ford began to supply kits to no fewer than 12 nations, as far flung as Australia and Trinidad, Pakistan and South Africa. In absolute terms, the CKD operation would never be very large, but it brought much local employment – and a real boost to the Transit's image – in every continent.

This, though, was merely the overture, to what became a non-stop performance. A new home, more sales, more derivatives – and a brand-new diesel power unit – were on the way.

Hot weather, cold weather, singly or in fleets, the original Transit found work. This was newspaper delivery in the snows of Sweden in the early 1970s.

3 Facelift time

By the early 1970s the British-built Transit had already out-grown its first home. Every day, and every shift, Langley was full and overflowing, and no further expansion was possible. Accordingly, it was deep-breath time – Ford had to find a new home for the project.

Fortunately, the solution was close at hand. Ford, expanding its facilities all round Europe, decided to take body pressing and assembly jigs out of the old Briggs factory at Southampton, re-equip it, and turn it into a dedicated Transit assembly plant. Starting in 1972, with a new assembly line building, the Southampton factory became the 'Home of the Transit' – and it still is, in the early 2000s.

It wasn't easy, of course – moving a complete assembly line never is – but it was done with amazingly little disruption. There was a slight overlap between the two plants – the first Southampton-built Transits appeared in late 1972, the last Langley-built models in the first weeks of 1973 – but in all other respects it was a clean break.

What happened to Langley after the Transit had left town? D-Series heavy-truck assembly was pushed rapidly upwards, and in due course the much-acclaimed Cargo took over. In 1986, however, the business was sold to Iveco-Fiat, and passed out of this history. Some later trucks built there still carried Ford badges, although the Dagenham connection is now long gone.

In the meantime, the market for small/medium diesel engines was gradually perking up, even at the more sophisticated end of the Transit market. At the time, the brutal truth for Ford was that the Perkins 4/108 engine had always struggled to be competitive, and the clientele was saying so, loud and clear. Perkins could do nothing, and showed no signs of making improvements.

Ahead of the game – as ever, at this point in their history – Ford saw this coming, saw that diesel-engined Transits would eventually become the norm, not the exception, and started its own design in the late 1960s. Charlie Baldwin, the go-ahead Vice President with truck responsibilities, was determined to have his own power unit, and got his way, and by mid-1971, was ready to preview a new range of straight-four/straight-six diesels. In Ford-speak, these were always known as the 'York' engines, and sales began in the first days of 1972.

But why 'York'? For no better reason than that Ford was using 'county' names for several such projects at the time, including 'Essex' for existing Transit petrol engines, 'Kent' for a small automotive petrol unit and 'Dorset' for a larger commercial diesel.

Ford, after all, has always loved its nicknames, and project codes – but it can get confusing at times. In the 1990s, a new-generation diesel engine for the Transit would be coded 'Puma', even though Ford was currently building a very smart little sports coupé badged as – Puma!

Until the 1970s, small diesel engines for cars and light truck use had always been heavy, low-revving and low-powered. The 'York' though, would be the first modern Ford diesel to change all that. Designed as a 2.3-litre four-cylinder unit (there was also a 3.5-litre 'six'), the more highly-rated of two versions developed 96lb ft of torque and produced 62bhp, which was a heartening advance over the 49bhp of the old Perkins 4/108 unit.

Looking back from the 2000s, where new diesel engines tend to have turbochargers, high-tech direct fuel injection by what is called 'common rail' plumbing, and produce the sort of mid-range torque which gives all gearbox designers nightmares, the 'York' of 1972 now seems puny by comparison. Then, however, it was hailed as a real advance.

Ford, who at the time seemed to be addicted to placarding facts and figures, claimed that no fewer than 150 prototype engines had been run, that they had collectively run for more than 50,000 hours, and that the engine was expected to boost diesel-engined Transit sales to well over 50 per cent of production. This claim by the way, was extra cautious, for the 50 per cent barrier was breached before the end of the 1970s, and within 20 years diesel-engined sales were running at 96 per cent of production!

No new engine, of course, is ever designed in isolation. The detail envelope of the 'York', therefore, had worked backwards from the space available in the Transit. Not only was it advertised as being 'small' (it might have weighed no less than 490lb (222kg), but it fitted into a box 24in long,

24in wide and 30in tall, but it was also installed under the bonnet with the cylinder block canted over to the left-side (i.e. near-side in the UK) of the Transit at 22.5°.

In overall packaging terms, this helped enormously. Because of the cylinder head cross-flow breathing arrangements, the exhaust manifold tucked down neatly under the left side, while the bulky inlet manifolds and (equally as important) the injector pump and electrical alternator lived high up, in the centre of the car.

Conventional in almost every way – it had a cast-iron block and head, five main crankshaft bearings, and Ricardo Mark VB-type pre-combustion chambers, with overhead valves prodded by push-rods – the 'York' drove its camshaft by internally cogged belt. Not quiet, not refined, but unashamedly beefy, it was a sturdy new engine of which Ford was proud. Not only

The '1978 ½' Transit received a reshaped nose, and would be built until 1986.

Southampton

Like Langley, the Southampton factory, now known in Britain as the 'Home of the Transit', once had a distinguished aircraft connection. The original factory was set up by Sir Hugo Cunliffe-Owen at Eastleigh Airport in the late 1930s.

Much expanded during the Second World War, it became one of several test and final assembly plants for the famous Supermarine Spitfire fighter aircraft, the last of which left the plant in 1946.

Taken over by Briggs Motor Bodies in 1949, the complex soon became a dedicated stampings plant. Vehicle body construction for Ford vans and trucks began in 1957 (these being supplied to Dagenham), and Ford took over the business in 1958.

By the 1960s Southampton was confined to body, paint and trim operations for vans and trucks, these being supplied to Langley. From 1965 to 1972, Southampton supplied every UK-assembled Transit body shell.

In a major expansion programme, a new final assembly building was erected, and Transit assembly was then concentrated at Southampton from late 1972.

British Transits were assembled at the modernised Southampton plant from 1972. This facelift production line view was taken in 1984, with assembly of the two millionth example just around the corner.

was it 25 per cent more powerful than the Perkins it replaced, but it could henceforth be used in the heaviest Transits of all.

Then, as later, Ford normally evolved the new engine to be used in many different models – cars and/or trucks – but in this case the four-cylinder 'York' was virtually dedicated to the Transit (and later, to the A-Series truck). Four years in the planning, it involved facilities being laid down at Dagenham, where a reputed £11.5 million had been spent.

At first, Ford expected to sell only about 30,000 'York'-engined Transits every year, but there was capacity for 50,000/60,000 units a year – and although a proportion of those were supposed to go out to industrial users, in practice, the Transit took whatever Dagenham could supply.

Although the weight penalty compared with the obsolete Perkins diesel was 90lb (41kg), none of the customers seemed to mind, especially as in 1972 this was now a £155 cost option compared with petrol-engined Transits. Typically, a 'York'-engined Transit 75 would cost a mere £982, while a 15-seat long-wheelbase bus sold for £1,637

'It was such a good engine,' Barry Gale told me, 'that Transits were sometimes stolen for their engine alone – and a number of them ended up as spares, or in boats!'

Onwards and upwards

Even before the new diesel engine appeared, the Transit had broken more records. The 500,000th example was built in 1971, and the three-quarter millionth would follow in 1974. In 1972, (the first year in which the 'York' diesel was available) no fewer than 100,000 Transits were produced for the first time in a year, of which 45,196 were sold in the UK. This was staggering proof of the way Ford's van had fastened on to every marketing opportunity.

It wasn't just that it could carry goods, but that it could carry people too. It wasn't just that it was available from Ford in so many different forms, but that a sub-industry could then offer scores of special conversions. Some special-converted Transits still looked recognisably like the products

Transit

which flowed out of Southampton and Genk in a never-ending stream, while others (like the Asquith 'vintage' buses, for instance) were almost unrecognisable. Police forces all over Europe bought them in big numbers, as did military and other security organisations. Luxuriously equipped buses? Of course. Breakdown trucks? Naturally. Self-advertising specials? Why not?

As far as Ford was concerned, building the Transit was certainly not a licence to print money, but it was always a very profitable operation – and the company's rivals made haste to develop their own similar models.

If there were clouds on the horizon, the Transit's team could not see them. Although the Energy Crisis of 1973/74 hit hard, Ford bounced strongly back. The team even found time to re-engine the 'starter' Transit in the UK, by dropping the lumpy old 1.7-litre V4 engine in favour of the lighter, more economical and very smooth 1.6-litre 'Kent' four-cylinder petrol engine – the same type which was already being used in Escorts, Cortinas and Capris.

'That was so low on torque,' one personality recalled, 'that we had to specify a 5.8:1 rear axle!'

Servo-assisted front disc brakes became

standard on all models at about this time, as did a minor front-end restyle, and the rejigging of the front cabin to provide more leg room. Ford's own C3 automatic transmission was finally added to the options list in 1977.

As the 1970s evolved, the Transit began to look a touch over-familiar to its clientele, but held its ground in the market place. Its

Ford finally revealed its brand-new 'York' diesel engine in 1972. This four-cylinder version was for use in the Transit, and there was also a straight-six for use in larger Ford trucks.

Fun and games on the banked track at the Monza motor racing circuit in Italy. Two 'York' diesel-engined Transits circulated for up to 10,000 miles at overall average speeds of 75mph in almost a week of non-stop action. Dirty? Well, yes, and you would be too if you hadn't had a wash for so long!

This, of course, not only involved adding a totally new type of driven front axle, but designing, engineering and developing a new main gearbox, complete with a centre differential. Then it was necessary to arrange for the forward propeller shaft to run up alongside the engine sump to the new front axle itself. Naturally, this meant that the entire body and chassis had to be raised to make provision for all this – as accompanying illustrations show.

Almost from the start of Transit 4x4 development, Ford struggled to make out an economic case for manufacturing such vehicles in any of its own factory plants, for the quantities forecast were small. Instead, it entered into co-operation with a specialist company – County Tractors Ltd (now Countytrac Ltd) – which carried out all the work under Ford supervision and control. This has proved to be a very fruitful partnership, which was still in existence well over 30 years later.

So, why did Ford not carry out such work itself? Barry Gale explained: 'There are two concepts of 4WD customers. Those who want enhanced traction (hotel shuttle buses in ski resorts, for instance) and those who want to take a lot of stuff, inside a van, off road, to the top of a mountain.

'The trouble with both types is that they might buy 50 of them from us, then not buy any more for the next ten years. Volumes tend to be very low …'

Asquith converted many VE6-style Transits into vintage pastiche vehicles. This open-top bus was based on the long-wheelbase chassis.

Ford also maintained close links with the BRSCC and Brands Hatch circuit. This 1978 Transit was used as a circuit ambulance, and gave many years of service.

UK share of its market sector, which had peaked at 45 per cent in 1970, rarely dropped below 37 per cent in the years which followed. Between 35,000 and 40,000 new Transits were delivered in the UK every year, this being a major proportion of Southampton production.

Although the millionth Transit was built on 15 September 1976, not even such a legend could be expected to go on indefinitely. It would have been wrong for Ford to assume that it could – for its own experience of the Model T had told it otherwise.

By this time, SVO had evolved a very ambitious up-grade of the basic specification – by developing a four-wheel-drive package.

Record *breakers*

When Ford introduced its 'own-brand' diesel, the 2.4-litre 'York', in 1972, it thought that a record-breaking endurance stunt would not go amiss. Accordingly, it sent two new diesel-engined Transits to the world-famous Monza motor racing circuit, where the banked track was still in existence.

In seven days and seven nights of non-stop driving, a short wheelbase van completed 6,215miles (10,000km) at an average speed of 75.0mph, while a 12-seater bus ran for 10,000 miles (16,090km), averaging 73.7mph. In both cases, stops were only made to refuel the Transits and to change the drivers.

Even so, it was not until March 1978 that any visual changes were made to this amazingly successful product. Ex-international and Olympic swimmer Graham Symonds, an accomplished stylist/feasibility designer, who became the Transit design chief in the 1970s, recalls just how simple those changes actually were: 'I facelifted the "oldie" with a new nose, new grille, and new rear lamps. Those were the days when we still worked on paper before transferring thoughts to clay – no computers at that time!

'Uwe Bahnsen was in overall charge of Ford design in those days, but in fact I was in charge of design work on the Cargo at the time [John Fallis was really in charge, but he was ill at home], and for the Transit work we had to build up a small team by "borrowing" them from some other car work.

'We regrilled and turn-indicator'd it, making a common nose – that was for the first time on the Transit, of course. In fact, when the original VE6 style [by a French company – see Chapter 4] was brought over for viewing, Bob Lutz thought that our facelift proposal still looked more modern than their all-new approach!'

Three instantly recognisable faces – HRH Princess Anne, three-times F1 World Champion Jackie Stewart, and a late-1970s-style Transit bus.

The police of many nations bought Transits in big quantities. This early 1980s facelift long-wheelbase Transit was in use as an accident unit by the Leicestershire Constabulary.

ONE MILLIONTH TRANSIT

THIS 2 LITRE BUS FOR NIGERIA IS THE ONE MILLIONTH TRANSIT TO BE PRODUCED *Ford*

The one-millionth Transit was assembled at Southampton in 1976, bound for Africa.

That, in fact, required less alteration than had originally been envisaged. Back in 1974 (and soon after the first energy crisis had struck) Ford had set up an advanced project team to work on a new van, the 'Triton' project.

This was scheduled to become a new Transit product line, and in the original engineering scheme of things it would have followed on once work on the new, larger, Cargo range had been completed, maybe one or two years later. In the end, practical and financial considerations as huge amounts of capital were being committed to the Cargo, and there were not enough engineers to complete both programmes, meant that the 'Triton' had to be sidelined.

(The 'Triton' name was revived for what became the VE6 of 1986, although this was very different to the previous model to carry the name.)

Evolution, not revolution

For Ford, in any case, this was a time for financial caution. The world-wide energy crisis of 1973/74 had hit the company very hard (the AVO factory, which had been producing high-performance Escorts, with a lot more already planned, was closed down,

for instance), the integration of British and German operations into Ford-of-Europe was going ahead very rapidly – and huge sums were being committed to the front-wheel-drive Fiesta project.

Maybe the time was right to start thinking about a Transit replacement – it would reach its tenth anniversary in mid-1975, of course – but as it was still selling fast (as the Americans would say: 'like 5 cent hamburgers …') there was really no need to make massive changes just to keep it in the showrooms.

Even so, Vice President Charlie Baldwin ('What a hands-on boss he was – he used to be down in the workshops every morning at 7 o'clock!') wanted to push through every change that Product Planning would allow. Working out of its new offices at Trafford House in Basildon, he pushed through the package of changes that included Symonds's styling update, with new engines and new equipment to match.

The visual update which reached the public in March 1978 was cleverly done. A new structure, with new panels ahead of the windscreen/bulkhead provided a nose that wrapped neatly around all the engines which

Ford was using, or even contemplating using. Having listened to its customers, Ford made it possible to unbolt the entire front panel and bumper, so that there was easy access to the engine bay.

Inside the cab there was a new fascia style, which looked much more car-like than before – one feature being a new three-spoke steering wheel. The main instruments had evolved from those of the best-selling Cortina. Where automatic transmission was fitted the change-speed quadrant was inboard of the driver's legs, on the floor. The transmission was now the Ford C3 type, as used in cars such as the Cortina and the Granada and although not many customers

Those were the days, when the mobile fish shop was a familiar sight in Britain's streets. This was a facelift Transit of the early 1980s.

In 1978, Radio Luxembourg, Europe's first commercial pop music station, used a Transit to move its roadshow around European cities.

A-Series

In the early 1970s, some years after the launch of the Transit, Ford launched another light truck range, called the A-Series. Although this machine looked rather similar to the Transit, there was little commonality – and nowadays no-one (at Ford, and certainly not at the dealerships) has happy memories of this.

Meant to fit in the marketing gap between Transit and the larger D-Series trucks, the A-Series used a modified version of the Transit cab on a conventional separate chassis frame. It used V4 *and* V6 petrol engines, plus four-cylinder and six-cylinder versions of the 'York' diesel engine.

Looking back, the A-Series offered no USP (unique selling proposition), was apparently a real rust-bucket, and was none-too-reliable.

As a project, it was a commercial failure, and unsurprisingly it did not survive into the 1980s.

Facelifted in 1978, the Transit now had a common nose, whether petrol or diesel engines were fitted. The structure and suspension were as solid and as technically simple as ever.

By the late 1970s, Transit fascia and instrument displays were much more car-like than the original models of the 1960s.

ordered this, there was enough demand to make it viable.

The biggest changes, however, were hidden away, for Ford chose this time to rejig the Transit's range of engines. The V4 engines around which the original Transit had been moulded were swept away, there were important improvements to the 'York' diesel, and a new overhead-camshaft straight-four petrol engine made its debut.

Ford-of-Europe, in fact, was finally rationalising its engines strategy. The old British 'Essex' V4 and V6s had already been dropped from the car range, in favour of German engines, although the V6 assembly tooling was transferred to Ford South Africa and lived on for many more years. The Transit had not used the 1.7-litre 'Essex' V4 since 1975, so now it was time to replace the 2.0-litre version.

Ford's latest corporate mid-sized petrol engine, an in-line 'four', single-overhead-camshaft power unit coded T88 (or 'Pinto', after its North American origins) was freely available and was an easy fit in the Transit engine bay. The 1.6-litre and 2.0-litre types were already being built in huge quantities, and providing enough power and torque was never going to be a problem. In private cars, 2-litre 'Pintos' produced up to 110bhp and redeveloping the engine for the Transit – to produce 65bhp (1.6-litre) or 75bhp (2-litre) was never going to be a problem.

'Maybe the T88 wasn't the obvious replacement,' Truck Development Manager John Packwood recalled, 'because it really wasn't the right sort of engine, because it didn't lug very well, and at first it didn't really have a reputation for longevity. We had many durability problems to solve with the Transit's accepted duty cycle.'

One major customer, incidentally, requested a super-economical version of the 2-litre 'Pinto', and was offered a 58bhp derivative, where power was reduced by fitting an inlet manifold restrictor close to the carburettor. This reminded Mike Hallsworth, who went on to become Vehicle Engineering Manager on new Transit projects, of the trouble he had once encountered when the British Post office requested a similar restricted-power 'Essex' V4: 'We used to call that restrictor the "mouse's ear", it was so tiny, and we linked it to a small venturi carburettor. It had

enormously tall gearing too. Amazingly, as a combination it worked! It was much more economical than the 1.6-litre "Kent" – but of course it wouldn't rev.

'The problem was that we demonstrated this Transit to the customer on a day when a lot more was being done on the test track. The customer tried out "his" Transit, and

From 1978, Ford dropped the old-style V4 engines and began using the more-recent, in-line, four-cylinder 'Pinto' engines instead. This was the first time an overhead-camshaft engine had been used in a Ford commercial vehicle.

The 'Pinto' engine used in the 1978-generation Transit had single-overhead-camshaft valve gear, which allowed revs to be much higher, if desired. This particular unit is a more highly tuned version, as used in a Ford private car.

France's much-feared CRS riot-control police chose Transits, not domestic French vehicles, when equipping their forces in the late 1970s.

Engineers from Ford built this floating Transit, to take part in the annual Maldon raft race.

found it was a lot more powerful than he expected. The problem was that one or our chaps had forgotten to fit the restrictor ...'

At the same time, changes were made to improve the 'York' diesel. When it originally went on sale an ether cold starting device was standard, but this was never satisfactory. Gordon Bird, who would later manage a massive new diesel engine project, had to arrange for glow-plugs to be added instead. For the '1978½' model these solved the cold-start problem, but had Ford's cost accountants jumping up and down at the expense of it all.

'Now,' Ford claimed, 'the "York" starts well in cold weather, all the way down to −20°C (−4°F) ...', which was important for customers in countries like Sweden, especially those who needed to deliver newspapers first thing in the morning of a gelid winter in Scandinavia.

Now, for the first time, the load of legislation to be passed was also increasing. 'Way back in 1965,' Gordon Bird told me, 'we had to meet a TUV brake test procedure, but that was all. In the 1970s we had to meet drive-by noise tests and smoke tests with the new diesel engine. A lot more followed.'

All this came along with an improved maintenance package, for services only had to be carried out at 12,000 mile (20,000km) intervals. Time spent off the road was always anathema to truck operators – to a private car owner, that might sound like making only a yearly visit to the garage – but for most Transit operators that meant a reduction in regular work of maybe four or five times a year.

Versatility

As before, one feature which made the latest Transit so attractive was that it could almost be tailored to an individual customer. The range of SVO options continued to grow, while majoring on well-proven kits like ambulance, welfare bus and caravan packages, police bus equipment, extended-wheelbase chassis/cabs, 4x4s, and more ...

'By that time,' Angus Macleod insisted, 'if a new customer came to us, asking for a particular feature, it was highly likely that we had already developed it, or even (unknown to him) made it available to another customer.'

With the Transit already being produced in ten locations (the most recently opened

This Transit was used in the Portuguese Grand Tour expedition, and is seen here in the Sahara Desert in 1982.

T88/'Pinto'
overhead camshaft
engine

Late in the 1960s, Ford developed a new family of four-cylinder engines, and arranged to have these built in the USA and in Europe. First announced in 1970, they were used in millions of Ford products over the next two decades.

Within Ford-of-Europe these engines would be known as the T88, whereas in the USA they were known as 'Pinto' types, as they were used in the new compact Ford-USA model of that name.

The T88/'Pinto' was the first Ford to have a single-overhead-camshaft cylinder head layout with the camshaft being driven by an internally cogged belt; the head itself was produced in cast iron.

Over the years, the European 'Pinto' was produced in 1.3, 1.4, 1.6 and 2.0 litre guise (which was done by juggling bore and stroke dimensions), and was employed in passenger cars such as the Escort RS models, the Cortina, the Taunus, the Capri and the Granada. It was used in the Transit, in 1.6-litre or 2.0-litre form, from 1978 to 1994.

Later in the 1970s, in the USA, the 'Pinto' engine was redesigned, enlarged to 2.3-litres and renamed 'Lima', but was still recognisably related to the original type.

factory having been in Amsterdam), sales jumped as a result of all this innovation. In only one year after 1978, Ford added 19,000 to its output from Southampton, and a further 19,000 from Genk, while output in Amsterdam leapt by 5,000. The accountants who had been worried about the cost of glow-plugs began to breathe again …

Even so, this was only a short respite. A year after the '1978½' model had been launched, the second world-wide energy crisis struck. The Shah of Iran was deposed,

Opposite *Rough-road testing at Ford's Boreham airfield proving facility.*

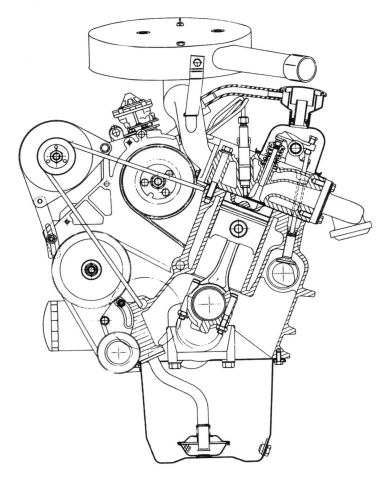

Ford introduced the direct-injection version of the 'York' diesel engine in 1984, not only enlarged to 2.5 litres, but with more power and considerably better fuel economy.

Islamic fundamentalism swept through the oil-rich nations of the Middle East, and oil prices surged yet again.

Ford soon realised that they would have to develop more fuel-efficient engines – not just in Europe, but all round the world. Among many new programmes, was the evolution of the DI (direct injection) diesel power unit which immediately replaced the 'York' diesel in 1984. In 12 years, incidentally, no fewer than 625,000 'Yorks' had been built.

This, Ford claimed, was the industry's first series production direct injection diesel.

Difficult to find this exciting, perhaps, but maybe as Ford was known as a technically cautious business at the time, this was a real act of faith, a real jump into the future. A new cylinder head eliminated the old-fashioned Ricardo pre-combustion chamber, high-pressure injection replaced the old type of low-pressure injection – and the glow-plugs could once again be abandoned. This time, Ford claimed, more than 100 prototype engines were built and tested – some of them, in secret, under the bonnet of favoured customers' vehicles.

This was so much so that, when Ford's new DI power unit was launched in 1984, many German media representatives commented that a rival organisation – Mercedes-Benz, no less – had recently assured them that high-speed direct injection was not feasible.

Ford, however, was not deterred. Direct injection worked well, of course, although not without some teething troubles. Even so, demand soon outstripped anything achieved by the original 'York' – so Ford was perhaps wise to lay down capacity at Dagenham to build up to 150,000 units every year:

'At the time,' project leader Gordon Bird recalls, 'there were people who wanted to keep the "York" name, but I wouldn't allow

that. The "DI" was something very different, and I wanted to emphasise that. Although some of the original tooling could be used, the only part carried over from the "York" was the rear cylinder block core plug!'

Not that this was a clean break, for Ford was not about to abandon the 'York' completely. Although the new engine's cylinder block was different, the casting could be remachined to make it compatible with service requirements.

Success was measured in the figures – 2.5-litres instead of 2.36-litres, 68bhp instead of 62bhp, and an improvement in fuel consumption which, at times, could reach over 24 per cent in the lighter-duty, short-wheelbase Transits.

In this case, by the way, the DI engine was so successful that it was eventually supplied for use in the legendary London taxi cab, and even in later years, for use by a nominally rival manufacturer, producing LDV (one time British Leyland) Sherpa vans.

Before the Transit reached another important anniversary – 20 years old in October 1985 – it also achieved an important milestone. On 25 July 1985, the two-millionth Transit of all was completed at Southampton, where it was greeted off the line by Ford Chairman Sam Toy, and the

noted botanist and 'green' campaigner, Dr David Bellamy.

But would the traditional Transit – the van which had become an icon, a symbol, a way of life, for so many people – ever need to be replaced? Ford thought it should, and in 1986 they announced the biggest improvement so far.

Maybe this Transit crew bus looks rather high off the ground …

… which is because it has been re-engineered with four-wheel-drive by Ford's SVO division.

4 VE6 – the second-generation Transit – 1986

By the early 1980s, outside Ford there were those who wondered if the company would ever have the nerve to produce a new type of Transit, but Ford staff never had any doubts. Even so, like British Leyland with the Mini, or VW with the Beetle, the original Transit had been so successful, so talismanic, so right for its job, and for such a long time that many efforts to replace it had been abandoned.

Even so, from time to time task forces were set up to study the Transit, the future of the product line, and what could be done about it. Way back in 1974, Ford considered developing a new model – which is when the original 'Triton' project name was chosen – but this was delayed, and delayed, and subsequently discarded in favour of the facelift programme instead. What followed in the 1980s was very different.

In the early 1980s, in any case, the Transit engineering team was only a small shadow of its former self, and for a time the company was reluctant to give approval to a new project on cost grounds.

'Finally,' John Packwood told me, 'and at the third time of asking, we got the programme approved. In one way this was a good thing, as it meant that it followed on from the heavy-truck Cargo project, which meant that resources and people had become available. Over at Trafford House, where we were, there were some super-egos!'

As a wry aside, Packwood told me that he managed the Body Engineering effort on the new model, and that the weight targets which he had to meet were extremely demanding. Peter Nevitt, who was running the entire project at the time, demanded that VE6 – which was bigger and more versatile than the Transit it had to replace – should be no heavier. Packwood thought it could not be done, so Nevitt challenged him: 'You mean that in 17 years of technology development in the Transit, you can't make the new model any lighter and stiffer than the old one?'

'Yes, that's *exactly* what I am telling you,' replied Packwood, 'because it's bigger, it's got a shed-load more glass, and we have been "thrifting" this thing for the last ten years. He was not happy about that … The targets were set very aggressively, but in the end, somehow, we met them.'

Graham Symonds, the designer who led the design of what became the VE6 (or 1986-model Transit), told me that original packaging and styling work began with an independent design house in France. This was under the guidance of Ford-of-Europe Truck VP Bob Lutz, and was so far back in history that (as noted earlier) work was eventually held over to allow the *original* Transit style to be facelifted!

Their effort, which even then was 'fast-fronted', but with a notch in the profile, was brought over to the Ford studios for Lutz to study. However, as already noted in Chapter 3, he did not like what he saw, and asked Symonds' team to produce their own alternative.

'Using the existing floorpan, we developed our own style,' Symonds says, 'Lutz took one look at it, and immediately cancelled everything with the French company. We looked at some of the competition, but found them so old-fashioned. We then worked very hard on the packaging, so that we made the shape feasible …'

In fact, the agreed shape was less sharp, somehow less extreme, than the original, but still retained its flavour. A choice had to be made between two-door/side-window profiles, but design is not just about shaping, but about practicability. Where would the door hinges go, where would the battery go, what about access to the engine bay? The fact that the floor/under-structure of the existing Transit was to be retained was another constraint, although on this occasion provision for fitting the Essex V6 in SVO applications was always considered.

It was, of course, totally and radically different from the '1978½' style which was already being built in huge numbers. Styling

and design feasibility work went on for some time, and it was up to two years before final approval was given.

When it was ready for launch in 1986, Ford knew that any advance in usage economics should be boasted. Proudly making one major claim – that with a drag coefficient of only 0.37, it had become the class leader, they pointed out that this more than balanced the larger size of the new-type shell. Overall fuel consumption, they promised, could be up to eight per cent better.

Incidentally, once this radical new style was out on test, I now know that General Motors designers somehow got hold of some spy photographs, and were so impressed by what they saw that a great deal of expense

VE6, the first completely new-style Transit since 1965, first appeared in 1986.

Early days in the design and shaping of the VE6 Transit, showing off an unfinished full sized clay model, and a rather severe shape of side window. This dated from the 1983 period.

When the VE6 was being engineered, several different types of rear door/hatch were considered, including a lift-up hatch.

and delay went into reworking new Opel-badged products which were underway.

While this was going on, Alan Selman became Manager of Advanced Light Truck Engineering in 1978, but it was never going to be quick and easy to turn any of these great ideas into reality. As Symonds has already confirmed, this was a project which took time to reach fruition.

From time to time, Alan's team had to be diverted to other truck-related projects, and it was not until 1982/83 that serious design work began on the 'Triton' project, which later gained the more familiar Ford acronym of VE6. By this time the size of the engineering had expanded mightily – this being necessary to meet all the burgeoning mass of safety and exhaust emissions

legislation for which the 1970s and 1980s were notorious.

Mike Hallsworth now takes up the story: 'Before then, we needed to find out just how Transits were being used in the real world. In the early 1980s we needed to replicate that, and Peter Nevitt got approval, because in the end this saved an awful lot of money on testing.'

The result was the setting up of a massive vehicle usage research programme. 'We sent out observers to sit in working Transits, and took thousands of observations of real-world customers driving their Transits. We used every engineer we could spare. They would note down how fast the Transit went, what roads and obstacles it was running over, what load it had on. Throughout the day the observers would note down the number of gear-changes, how many times the van was loaded and unloaded, how often it was fully loaded, how much reversing was involved, how much heavy braking took place, and how often full-lock turns were used.

'Then, after analysis, we were able to programme computers that controlled durability rigs, so that we could run a test in three weeks which would have taken three months of running on the road. We could also build up standard test procedures of our own. We don't think that any of our competitors ever did this – not even our colleagues in the USA, by the way.

'It worked excellently. We built up a tremendous data-base on how Transits were being used – not just in Britain, but in

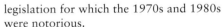

Germany, Italy, Sweden and more – so eventually we knew just what we had to engineer for, and test for. One thing we learned, for instance, was just how much "kerbing" a Transit was put through.'

All this work, and the planning which went alongside it, meant that the new product, when it came, would be a quantum leap ahead of the '1978½' model that it would replace.

Which, of course, it had to be, for Ford's rivals had steadily been catching up for some time. When the new-generation Transit VE6 was finally launched in January 1986, Britain's *Commercial Motor* magazine made this very astute summary: 'When you are the most successful van manufacturer in Britain, replacing your top-selling model is a risky business. Should the new model be revolutionary, or simply evolutionary?

'This is the problem Ford has had to face. However, after six years' research and development, and investment of nearly £400 million (£100 million alone of which has gone into modernising its Southampton van plant) Ford has finally launched the new Transit.

'The latest Transit must succeed if the company is to retain its current massive 30 per cent market share …'

History now tells us that Triton/VE6 *was* a great success, and sold just as well as hoped. The original Transit had been in production for just over 20 years, and the Triton/VE6 family would go on, not quite to match this, but to enjoy a life of 14 years.

Except that modified versions of existing petrol and diesel engines (and their related transmissions) were carried over, and that much of the existing underbody/chassis layout was retained, many other aspects of the new van range was new. Not only was there a new style and a new package, but the wheelbases (short *and* long) had been

Small Transit VE6, or large driver? Capital Radio's 'Mile Muncher' circled the newly completed M25 motorway for seven days and seven nights. With several driver changes, we hope …

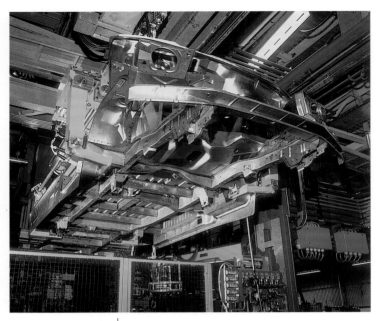

This underbody view of an early-type VE6 body shell taking shape shows the immensely strong underside of all Transits.

By the 2000s, Richard Parry-Jones was Ford's world-wide, top-ranking, technical officer, but he still remembers, with pride, his part in developing the original VE6. Richard is standing third from the left in this 1985 group shot.

that they could start digging huge holes in the floor, as big as Olympic swimming pools, parallel to the existing lines …'

In theory, though, and always as an aim, Ford wanted to retain the existing underbody, simply to cut the time, effort and investment needed to develop a new model:

'In fact, we kept on grading all the changes in terms of performance and manufacturing savings. A classic example – we actually retooled the LCY, long-wheelbase, longitudinal chassis members, though you wouldn't see the difference. We worked through the whole car that way, by co-operating closely with the manufacturing people.'

This was also the time when a very important Ford character enters this story – Richard Parry-Jones, who in the 1990s, would go on to be the most senior engineer in the entire world-wide Ford empire: 'The first time I met with Transit, I had just graduated, and Ford offered me a job in Vehicle Engineering, but I didn't like that, played hard to get, and turned them down. Eventually I joined the engineering division to work on cars.

'Years passed by, then Ron Mellor asked me to move from Car Product Planning to Engineering. But because there wasn't any promotion in that, I turned him down. Soon afterwards, I was asked to be Product Planning Manager for the Transit *and* Sierra P100 pick-up product lines.

'Someone was needed to look to the future, and not be distracted by the launch of models close to production. So although I was definitely a truck "greenhorn", I took that job. Even so, I found it rather

stretched, and a cleverly detailed type of independent front suspension had also been adopted – but only on the short-wheelbase/lighter payload types at first.

'When we started the job,' Packwood says, 'the assumption was that we were not planning to alter the factories very much, which meant that there would be the same number of stations on which to build the Transit. At first, therefore, there was a huge amount of component carryover from the old [1978½] model. In the end, though, the only underside panel that we didn't modify in some way was the centre rear floor!

'And the factories were completely re-equipped! We had to commit to certain aspects a year earlier in the programme than usual, so

frustrating, because after the VE6 had been launched, finance allocated to the cycle plan for on-going Transit work wasn't very big.

'As it turned out, I also got involved in VE6 quite a bit. The great thing, for me personally, was that in this time I learned a lot about the truck business. Transit was a fascinating study, and as everyone else has no doubt pointed out, it has a pretty unique history.

'While I was there, for quite a long time we worked on a 4.5-tonne Transit – a Transit with a 3-tonne payload. We weren't able to make sense of that – one reason was that we'd just suffered a disaster with the A-Series, and another is that the size of the market didn't develop in the way we had forecast. The 4.5-tonne Transit would really have replaced the A-Series, but it would have been longer, but the biggest challenge was to get the frame upgraded to deal with the payload.

'We built one or two, and had them on test, but I could never make out a good enough business case ...

'I was only in the Transit team for two to three years, then I was moved out – but I never lost touch with Transit. At that time, incidentally, engineering talent and engineering correctness was more highly valued in trucks than in cars, and many people stayed with trucks because they enjoyed it so much.

'I went off to America after that, then years later I came to run Ford-of-Europe Engineering at Cologne in 1991. That's when Transit came back into my orbit – Mike Hallsworth was my engineering manager on Transit. The big difference then, and later too, was that whereas all car vehicle engineering had been centred in Germany, in Cologne, the Truck project was always British-based ...'

Since that time, of course, Richard has risen to the loftiest height of all at Ford, but has never lost touch with Transit – or with the people who run the programmes.

Engineering

Grafting a new independent front end to an existing underframe and structural front end was very carefully and cleverly done. Heavier/longer-wheelbase Transits were to retain the old under-floor and the simple

'My name is Michael Caine.' The Transit VE6 also had a role in the 1987 film Fourth Protocol, *chasing Pierce Brosnan as the villain.*

One of the Transit VE6's most proud successes was to be chosen by Britain's flagcarrier airline, British Airways, to provide crew buses and many other derivatives of the design.

When designing independent front suspension for the new-generation VE6, Ford had to choose between this classic MacPherson strut layout …

… or this modified MacPherson installation, where the top of the strut was much more compact than usual, and the coil spring was inboard. The aim was to provide more foot space close to the wheelarch pressing.

beam/leaf-spring layout of earlier Transit models until the early 1990s.

'Even at this stage,' Packwood insists, 'we had wanted to increase the length of the longer wheelbase, but we could never make a business case for that, and we had to accept a compromise.'

After a lot of analysis, not only theoretical and practical, but also financial, the underframes of independent and beam-axle

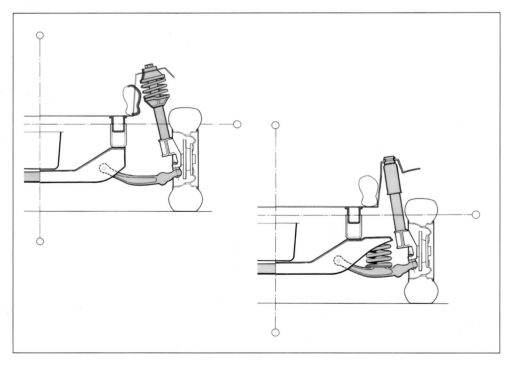

types were made common. This was important, not only because of the way it reduced costs and complications, but because manufacturing plant jigging and locations all revolved around the use of the front spring pivot. Beam-axle VE6s tied their leaf springs to that point, while on other VE6s the sub-frame supporting an independent front end also fastened to the same point – clever!

Much of the engineering and development effort went into the design of the new independent front suspension (IFS). Although this would be a costly improvement over the simple beam axle ('I-beam' in Ford-speak), extensive market analysis had already shown that Ford's credible rivals were already moving in the same direction.

(Rivals who refused to embrace independent front suspension all saw their sales shrivel away – the ex-BMC/ex-British Leyland/LDV range, which retained an I-beam layout into the 2000s being a perfect example.)

Part of that analysis included a poll of Ford's truck dealers, but this partially misfired. When asked if they wanted IFS on a new model, apparently 40 per cent of them replied that they thought the Transit already had it as standard!

Ford's system, designed not only to provide better handling and a better ride, was also inevitably to weigh more, and to cost more than before. However, it was so carefully and cleverly done that Alan Selman gained an award from the company for the work he carried out, as it was so technically novel. Although Ford always described it as a MacPherson strut layout (and the geometry, indeed, was identical), there were important differences.

On a conventional MacPherson system, the long, near-vertical, damper/strut is surrounded by a coil spring. This, by definition, is quite bulky at the top end where it is screwed to the bodywork. On the new VE6, however, the damper stood alone, with the short coil spring mounted inboard.

This was done presumably, for packaging reasons: 'We wanted to keep the top of the strut very slim,' Selman confirmed. 'It was not just because we wanted to keep the engine bay wide, but because we needed more space for the passengers' feet. In a semi-forward control layout like this, the driver's and passenger's feet are between the wheelarches – not ahead of them, or well behind them – so we needed to squeeze every millimetre out of the package to give more space.

Behind every famous car … there is often a fleet of Transits. When Ford's 'works' team of Sierra RS Cosworths set off to compete in the 1987 Finnish Rally of 1000 Lakes, the rally cars were supported by a new fleet of specially kitted-out Transit VE6s, which would go on to serve the team for some years.

The Transit chassis/cab unit could turn its hand successfully to almost anything. This Cambridgeshire-based VE6 delivers a load of Norfolk reed for a rethatching project.

'Ford has a convention regarding the space to be allowed around a wheel – it covers bump, rebound and steered wheel/tyre movement limits. On VE6, to get the wheelarch shape as compact as possible, we put the largest tyres we would use on to a "mule" and packed the underside of its wheelarch pressings with quick-setting polystyrene foam.

'I then told the test drivers to belt the **** off the "mule", to hit kerbs as hard as they dared, to drive flat out on pot-holed tracks – just run it to death – but bring it all back in one piece – just.

'Well, the tyres carved away the polystyrene, and from what was left we got a very realistic profile of what the vehicle actually had to cope with. That allowed us to reduce the wheelarch pressing "envelope" to the smallest possible size, and still have no problems. It took time to convince management why this should be so, and

Selman had to present his findings all the way up to his director, Peter Nevitt. Fortunately, two drawings which Selman prepared for his briefing paper have survived, and these tell their own story, and are reproduced here.

Even so, it had not been a simple choice, for the merits of what Ford call an SLA (short long arm – a wishbone layout to the layman), and of the twin swivelling I-beam layout as used in Ford-USA light trucks, had also been investigated.

Take one Transit chassis-cab, add a neat dust cart conversion – and in the 1990s scores of local authorities were content.

A great publicity show – with a VE6-style Transit converted for use as a competition car tug – the car, of course, being the fabulous four-wheel-drive RS200.

An added complication was that the team also adopted non-assisted rack-and-pinion steering with the new modified MacPherson strut front end, yet kept the old-type recirculating ball steering for the heavyweight beam-axle types – and were obliged to preserve a common steering column shaft so that there would be no differences in bulkhead/firewall instrument panel packaging:

'We got round that,' Selman told me, 'by having a common upper column, and a joint in the engine bay which linked the two different steering installations in two different directions.'

The sleek new style hid a smooth Granada-type fascia/instrument panel, and a front seating area which was more car-like than ever before. With a lot more glass – compared with the original type, the windscreen was huge, and the driver also had a much better view out of the side windows – the new machine looked dramatically more modern.

Except that the puny old 1.6-litre overhead-valve 'Kent' petrol engine was long gone, the line up of power plants was much the same as before. The vast majority of new Transits would be ordered with the latest

direct injection diesel engine, rated at 68bhp, with a minority powered by overhead-camshaft 'Pinto' or even (SVO applications only) the gallant old 3.0-litre V6 'Essex', which was imported from South Africa .

(So much of the new VE6 was carried over, or only lightly modified, from the existing model that one wag said: 'If we coded the original Transit the "Redcap", why don't we call this one the "Re-cap"?')

Maybe Ford was still being somewhat cautious over its engine supply policy (some testers moaned that there was not enough low-speed torque in petrol engines, and not enough top-end power in diesels), but with the order books continuing to build, the company didn't lose too much sleep over this.

The big change in the drive line came immediately behind the engines, where a five-speed all-synchromesh manual gearbox (based on that of the latest Sierras and Granadas) became optional on all but the 1.6-litre petrol engined types.

The arrival of this new model, incidentally, virtually coincided with a major corporate sell-off, when Ford and Iveco (a Fiat subsidiary) agreed a deal whereby Iveco bought the Langley plant, along with the rights to the larger Cargo model. This was the point at which Ford's 'Truck Operations' division really ceased to exist. One consequence, too, was that the SVO was obliged to leave Langley, and to re-settle in offices at Dunton.

'I was instantly moved out of Heavy Truck, into the SVO operation,' Angus Macleod remembers.' The move took two to three months. We had to find space to work, find out how Dunton worked, welcome other team members, move all the drawings from Langley to Dunton, and set up relationships in Dunton!'

This sale had been rumoured for some time, but most Ford men hoped that it would never happen. Even so, the disbanding of the British Truck Engineering group was brutally handled. Immediately after the sale, Mike Hammes gathered the staff together for a pep talk, delivering a speech promising a rosy future. After getting a standing ovation for this oration, he left the company a few days later!

Peter Nevitt was left to pick up the pieces as best he could, and save as many jobs as he could, for the heavy truck team found themselves with nothing to do, then Nevitt soon moved out as well, and for a time the Transit team was quite rudderless. As Hallsworth remembered: 'We were then absorbed into the bowels of Car Product Development. What was left of the Transit

team, we were almost wiped out. We could do small stuff, but nothing serious for future models. After VE6, suddenly there was nothing in the pipeline, there was just a blank void.'

Launch

Right from the start, when the VE6 was introduced in January 1986, it made a tremendous impression on the market place. Not only did it look smarter, with an improved package, and was available in even more versions, but with independent front

In the 1980s, automatic transmission was always optional on the Transit. This VE6 model has the then latest four-speed derivative fitted.

A version for all uses – this being a 'double cab' model of the VE6, with two rows of seats, but only the usual number of doors.

suspension the short-wheelbase derivatives had a much better ride and handling.

Once again, to quote *Commercial Motor*: 'Given Ford's enormous experience at building a market-dominating – indeed, market-shaping – van, it would be surprising if the new Transit turned out to be a dud … The new Transit does not match the great leap forward which its predecessor represented in 1965, but on the evidence so far it is good enough a mid-1980s van to remain the benchmark in the market.'

The press, in other words, had picked up the vibrations which were already coming from the marketplace – that the new model looked startlingly different from the old, was

This was the original type of SWB VE6 van, powered by the 2-litre overhead-camshaft 'Pinto' engine. In its basic format, this van would be built for the next 14 years.

The Southampton plant has always prided itself on being the 'Home of the Transit', and had recently built this 1990 model.

still just as versatile as its predecessor and looked set to maintain its huge lead in Britain and other territories.

In styling at least, the latest Transit was a quantum leap forward from the range it was replacing, and the public – whether business or private – loved what they saw. The old '1978½' model had sold well and steadily, on an established reputation, but certainly not on what it looked like. Functional rather than smart, it had delivered on the balance sheet, rather than on the styling front.

At a stroke, therefore, the new 'fast-front' VE6 variety changed all that. To the existing bottom line figures – price, payload, versatile options, durability, and established reputation – Ford now added the inestimable asset of styling. By moving to the new shape, the company had lost nothing (the VE6, in fact, was a more functional package than ever before), but had picked up extra points by being ultra-smart too. One needs to do no more than look at the shape of a Transit bus, and to compare the old with the new shape.

It was the market place which confirmed this at once. Soon after the new, smoothly styled 'fast-front' VE6-type Transit hit the streets in 1986, sales took off in an amazing manner, as the public all over the world seemed to love what it was offered. Only 38,900 Transits had been built at

Southampton in 1985 (the year before VE6 appeared), yet in 1989 that figure had doubled to 78,500. At Genk, the surge was even more dramatic – from 37,200 in 1985 to a massive 84,200 in 1989.

World-wide, no fewer than 173,059 Transits were built in 1989. This was a new company record by any standards, and in the UK, Ford was well on its way to selling its millionth Transit – a landmark which would be reached in 1991.

Nothing, however, kills like complacency, and Ford was not about to fall into that elephant trap. New regulations seemed to be coming at the Transit from all angles, and Ford's rivals were finally catching on to the appeal of this amazingly versatile product. Gordon Bird's team worked hard at the modern 2.5 DI diesel engine, finally introducing a second-generation design in 1988, with exhaust emissions much reduced and the power actually creeping up a little, to 70bhp. The Transit's early days, when it could only offer an anaemic (and smoky) 41bhp diesel engine, were long gone.

Perversely, however, early in the 1990s the transport world moved smartly into recession and sales fell off the edge of a cliff. Fortunately though, Ford, was almost too busy to notice and yet another major update to this much-loved icon was on the way.

Purely by chance, they assured us, Ford 'caught' this new-model VE6 Transit driving past Southampton, 'Home of the Transit', on the M27 motorway in early 1986.

5 VE64 and VE83 – maturity in the 1990s

Five years on, and in spite of the lull which followed the launch of the new-generation Transit, Ford was able to update this vehicle once again. Purely by chance, this came at exactly the right time, for all over Europe sales of such vehicles had begun to fall rapidly. The boost in sales which followed the novelty of a new model was welcome.

Casual observers, however, might not even have realised that the Transit which Ford always knew as the VE6 had been up-graded into a new type, known internally as the VE64. Visually, in fact, most people would have picked out the 'softer' profile to the headlamps, but they would certainly not spot the difference in wheelbase. They would, in other words, certainly struggle to realise that the two types were at all different.

Yet there were several major advances, one being that the VE64 featured a largely new underbody assembly aft of the cab, others being that the wheelbase of the long-wheelbase type was much longer than ever before, and all versions were now to be built with independent front suspension. Plus, these were new engines, new interiors and a raft of equipment upgrades …

Against the odds

In a good fairy story, everything to do with this particular programme would have been smooth, well-planned and logical, but as already noted, at Ford in the late 1980s the commercial vehicle side of the business was in considerable turmoil.

After Ford had sold off its heavy truck interests to Iveco-Fiat, its truck engineering team at Trafford House in Basildon was speedily decimated, its forward programme was disrupted, and only a rump of experienced staff remained to look after the Transit and its developments. Peter Nevitt, for instance, who had directed the VE6 programme, moved over to Iveco, taking some staff with him.

Although this certainly did not show in the production figures at Southampton, Genk and Azambuja (Portugal), as well as Turkey, which had risen in total from 111,500 in 1986 to 167,400 in 1989, it showed up in the strain placed on those who stayed behind. When Rod Hammonds took over as Programme Director in 1988, the future challenges for Transit were already obvious.

'I had no truck knowledge behind me at this time,' Rod now admits, 'it was a steep learning curve for me. However, many of my staff had worked there for many years, and knew a lot more about the business. When I arrived, what we now know as VE64 was still only an advanced programme at that stage.'

Ford's staff had been thinned down so much by this time that there were simply not enough bodies to successfully push a new derivative through to the marketplace, so this was when KBD, a local engineering contract concern, was drafted in to provide assistance. As it transpired, they would provide the vast majority of the man-hours needed.

Not that this was ever going to be easy. Because Ford originally found it difficult to liaise with an outside contractor (this was the Transit group's first experience of such an arrangement), KBD was invited to come into the yawning empty spaces of Ford's Trafford House building where they took over the top floor.

'One of the curious things about the Transit programme,' says Hammonds, 'was that it was always very profitable – every time management resisted spending on Transit, we used to remind them that it made 90 per cent of Ford's European profits from only about 10–15 per cent of the volume. This always encouraged management to leave us alone; we could more or less run our business as we saw fit.'

Eric Hoile, who had been a young development engineer on the original Transits, also began to take a more important role, and was soon to be heavily involved: 'I'd been working on Ford heavy truck development for years, but after that business was sold off to Iveco, I returned to working on Transit. I was in transmission engineering and I remember first getting closely involved with the development of the four-speed automatic transmission, matched to the 85bhp diesel-engined vehicle.'

These were the principal characters in the next phase of Transit development, and although the resulting product, VE64, would only have a separate life of three years (1991–94) it was eventually clear that it had been a vital link in the development chain.

Although the 1992 Transit (which was introduced in October 1991) known as VE64 looked virtually unchanged, much had been altered under the surface. The fact that the longer of the wheelbases had been enlarged

'Smiley-face', internally coded as VE83, went on sale in 1994.

Formula 1 driver Heinz-Harald Frentzen, a Sauber-Ford star in the mid-1990s, using a VE83 model promoting a 1996 campaign against drinking and driving.

Vintage? No – brand new in the late 1990s, but built on a Transit base.

by a massive 21.6in (550mm), and the rear underfloor had been upgraded to meet the latest crash test regulations meant that there was effectively a totally new underpan – at least, behind the line of the cab.

Even back in the mid-1980s, when good profits seemed easy to make, life for the Transit had never been easy: 'VE6 had had a difficult birth,' Hammonds reminded me, 'with a lot of cost constraints. But when we started looking at developments for VE64, it was obvious that the old-type twin-rear wheels, and wide wheelarches, were still a

big limitation. This was beginning to make the Transit uncompetitive.'

It was time for a major rethink of everything which, to the observer, was out of sight and out of mind, although to the engineers and those who had to oversee Ford's compliance with new regulations, it was vitally important.

The basic moves were to upgrade the structure in the nose, to specify independent front suspension for long as well as short-wheelbase Transits, and to lengthen the wheelbase of the longer-wheelbase type, and eliminate the need for twin rear wheels on heavily laden types. As one of the hard-working team said many years later: 'After doing the VE6, this was really like sweeping up unfinished business …'

At the time, Ford made much of the need to keep abreast of new legislation, claiming that the revised structure 'not only improved manufacturing efficiency and thus build quality, but also allowed these models to handle the full force of a 30mph barrier crash test, and provide the strength required to restrain even a triple seat and its occupants. The front end structure, seat-belt anchorages, seat mountings and the seats themselves were also reinforced to satisfy the test requirements. The [new] underbody

design allowed a new 1½ tonne payload SWB Model, the Transit 150, to be introduced on 15in wheels.'

'The VE64, in fact, didn't really change anything forward of the B-pillar [the pillar behind the passenger doors], but the underbody was new behind the doors,' Mike Hallsworth told me. 'In that area, all that really changed was that the chassis side rails themselves were improved, and the floorpan/load floor was extended, as the axle was moved backwards. We wanted to get rid of twin rear wheels, because that would let us fit much slimmer inner wheelarches. That meant that we could increase the width of the load floor, which was very important.'

In fact, the changes brought in for the VE64 were really completing the job that VE6 had started in 1986. Although this was a long-planned development, and had been completed with an eye to adding versatility and enhancing the safety performance of the structure, there were other benefits. On the longer-wheelbase types, where the back axle line had been pushed back much closer to the tail of the body, this finally allowed single, instead of twin, rear wheels to be adopted. Accordingly, this then allowed the width of the inner wheelarches to be reduced considerably, and given flat tops. In that

location, the width of the loading floor was therefore increased by 14.4in (365mm) to 54.2in (1,376mm); crafty!

But this was only one part of a package of changes which, without really increasing the overall size of the vehicle, made the Transit into a more attractive commercial proposition. This was the time, the engineers concluded, when the model could be offered with a six-year anti-perforation warranty – this obviously being important for all commercial users whose Transits operated in mud-slush and every other combination of nasty conditions.

[The Transits which were used deep underground – 500 feet below the surface – in the salt mines under Cheshire, must have had the hardest time of all. Such machines, incidentally, could not be delivered to ICI as completed vehicles, but were sent down as partly assembled kits, and finished off by Ford technicians. When they came to the end of a long and arduous life they were abandoned and entombed on site. At one time, ICI was operating up to 16 Transits in this way, in 20 square miles of tunnels and caverns. None of them would ever be brought back to see the sunlight and so one day an archaeologist is going to make an intriguing discovery down there.

This was the VE64, 1991-variety of the long-wheelbase Transit with a new, stiffer and more crash-resistant underbody, a longer wheelbase than ever before, now with single rear wheels, narrow inner wheelarch pressings, and a turbocharged version of the direct-injection 2.5-litre diesel engine.

Ever since 1965, Transits have been used deep underground in Britain's only salt mines, in Cheshire. They were too large to be lowered underground in one piece, so were sent below in partly dismantled condition, and reassembled on site. When finally worn out, they were buried – to present a real challenge for future archaeologists to work out! This 1985 line-up shows several generations of Transit.

This might just be the noisiest Transit in the world, for the roof, walls and floor were lined with 50mm of concrete, the better to support 65 amplifiers and 61 sub-woofer speakers, which belted out 155dB.

Under the nose, it was time to add modified MacPherson strut independent front suspension to the longer-wheelbase model instead of the old beam front end, this being almost the same IFS (although beefed up) as that already in use on shorter machines. At the same time, rack-and-pinion steering was standardised on all types.

The single rear wheel package, which came with 15in road wheels, was obviously an important cost *and* bulk saving, which must have offset the decision to specify ventilated front disc brakes, bigger rear drums and technologically complex four-channel anti-lock ABS braking as an option.

The engine line-up was considerably enhanced. Not only was this the moment to introduce a turbocharged version of the direct-injection diesel power unit, but to upgrade all the normally-aspirated engines too. Starting with VE64, only two basic engines were on offer – the well-known diesel and the gallant old overhead-cam 'Pinto' petrol engine.

SVO options, of course, continued as before – for Angus Macleod of SVO recalls seeing a few Ford-Germany V6 engines with modified gear ratios, being fitted (the old 'Essex' V6 engine was no longer available). 'In many ways that was the most complex jobs which SVO tackled, I think, because we had to rework the entire chassis, brakes and so on at the same time.'

In the same period, a few customers asked if the ambulance package could be made even smoother by the use of automatic transmission. 'Standard Transits', as ever, were very rare.

The vast majority of all such Transits were now diesel powered, either with the normally aspirated 70bhp or 80bhp DI unit, or with the lusty new 100bhp turbocharged

derivative. This was a major advance – Ford claimed 42 per cent more power and 52 per cent more torque compared with the diesel fitted to the VE6, which was going to make a phenomenal difference to the performance – all linked to new 'clean' tuning, and with self-monitoring electronic ignition and engine management systems.

Compare this sort of installation with that originally made in the Transits of the mid-1960s, and see just how far light truck design had advanced in 26 years.

Petrol engines, too, were more powerful than before, with 87bhp or 96bhp, and there was no longer any attempt to provide any super-economical/low-power derivatives. Past experience had shown that all such engines might satisfy one customer for one particular task, but were rarely popular in the general marketplace.

This, incidentally, did not only apply to trucks – for Ford had found the same when offering super-economy engines in some of its passenger cars. As a public-spirited exercise, and as a headline-forming act, it always sounded promising, but it never translated into extra sales.

For everyone at Ford who was operating with limited resources, and seemingly without enough support from top

In 1991, when the VE64-style Transit was introduced, Ford also specified a new type of petrol engine, the single-cam 'Pinto' 2.0-litre being equipped with electronic fuel injection. This power unit had already been fitted to Sierra and Granada/Scorpio private cars. By any standards, this was high-tech stuff, but the basic premise of the Transit, as a rugged, long-life load-carrier, was never lost.

For this early VE83, the picture says it all.

Transit

management, the new VE64 range was an impressive achievement. As usual, there was a wide choice – with engines from 70bhp to 100bhp, two wheelbases, payloads spanning 1,753lb (795kg) to no less than 4,029lb (1,827kg), and with a mind-boggling array of body styles.

At the time, therefore, it was no wonder that Ford boasted of spending £300 million in new investment, and in completing 2,500,000 miles of test, development and endurance driving before bring this new derivative to market.

Yet it was certainly worth it. To quote one admiring source: 'The Transit has the advantage of being all things to all men (and women); from the ground up it is designed purely as a light commercial vehicle, not as a car with a diverse model range including a van. *It's been Britain's best-selling commercial vehicle for a quarter of a century.*' (The italics are mine, but the point was well made.)

It was enough to keep the cash registers ringing, to keep the special versions chiming in, and enough to keep the production lines active. At Southampton, production rose from 54,500 in 1991 to 66,300 in 1994 (by which time this plant was always operating close to capacity), while at the more expansive plant

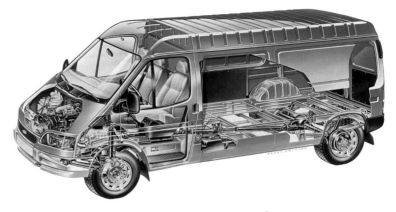

at Genk in Belgium, production held steady in the 70,000 to 75,000 region.

On 6 September 1994, and even as the VE64 model was being overtaken by a revised version, the three millionth Transit of all was produced, this time in Genk. A measure of Transit success is that it had taken only nine years to manufacture that third million, and with demand rising all the time, Ford gleefully continued to plan for the future.

Smiley face VE83

The final tweak of this successful second-generation design came in September 1994,

The Transit got a 'smiley-face' grille in 1994, like other Ford passenger cars of the period, although the engineering was still based on that of the VE6.

VE83 models shared the same basic 'smiley-face' nose as many Ford private cars of the day.

Ford's resourceful SVO department had much to do with idealising the Transit for use by the Australian postal service.

Early in the 1990s, Ford-of-Europe's designers had decided to evolve a new corporate 'face' for all its products, the result being that an oval grille, which became known as the 'smiley face', was adopted for its products.

This makeover worked better on some types than others – the smile looked good on the Transit and the Escort, reasonable on the Fiesta, but was rather disastrous on the final-type Scorpio. Product planners, marketing men and image specialists, though, like that sort of thing – so the Transit fell into line.

At the same time, through-flow ventilation was provided by grilles high on the rear quarters. Commercial users, too, noted that the new Transit would normally be provided with unglazed rear doors, a change which had been requested so that casual thieves would not immediately realise what was being carried. To balance the loss of driver's rear visibility, the door mirrors were made much larger.

By this time, Mike Hallsworth had moved smoothly up to become Vehicle Engineering Manager on the Transit line and had Eric Hoile alongside him, but still found that he

when VE64 gave way to VE83. This was the final derivative of a long-running 'traditional' light truck layout, for the new-generation Transit, which followed six years later, in 2000, would be almost totally different.

Transits don't come much more monster than this. Weighing 6.5 tonnes, 'Sky High' was, once a VE83, used axles from a US military personnel carrier, and an automatic transmission from a London bus.

Transit

Twin-overhead-**camshaft** *engine*

To replace the old T88/'Pinto' power units, Ford evolved a new family of four-cylinder engines in the late 1980s, which would be built at Dagenham. Intended to be more powerful, quieter, and to have much 'cleaner' exhaust emissions than the supplanted engines, these were twin-overhead-camshaft types with aluminium cylinder heads, these cams being driven by chain. Originally they were built either as two-valves-per-cylinder ('8-valve') or four-valves-per-cylinder ('16-valve') types, and would eventually be used as 'north-south (in-line) or 'east-west' (transversely-mounted) engines, for cars with rear-wheel-drive, front-wheel-drive or even four-wheel-drive.

In the passenger car range they found homes, variously, in the Sierra, Granada/Scorpio, Escort and Galaxy ranges of the 1990s and 2000s. Originally as 1,998cc, they were produced in carburettor or fuel-injected form, while later types of 2,295cc were always fuel-injected. The 8-valve type was used in the Transit VE83 from 1994, the 16-valve type in the new-generation Transit from 2000.

The most powerful 16-valve/2.0-litre unit was rated at 150bhp, and was used in the Escort RS2000. This engine, incidentally, could be power-tuned to between 280bhp and 300bhp for use in motorsport.

To make it smoother for use as a front-wheel-drive engine in the Galaxy MPV, and in the Scorpio, the 2,295cc engine was treated to an ingenious twin balance-shaft conversion, where the shafts were mounted in the sump, underneath the line of the crankshaft, and were driven by chain.

---

and his department simply could not cope with the explosion of work required.

The new nose in fact signalled, and hid, a whole raft of technical changes.

'I had been away from the Transit for some years,' Richard Folkson recalls, 'until suddenly I was brought back in as Project Manager on the new type (VE83) at Christmas 1992. Fundamentally this revolved around slotting the modern twin-overhead camshaft petrol engine into the existing structure.'

Fitting a twin-cam engine into a commercial vehicle might sound flamboyant (Alfa Romeo had been doing it for decades, of course), but Ford had little choice, as its European armoury of power units was changing fast. The old T88/'Pinto' engine was about to be killed off, and this new DOHC (double overhead camshaft) unit had already taken over in private cars. Although the DOHC was a Dagenham-built engine, it was quite a lot more expensive to make than the old T88. The new DOHC, however, was not only more powerful, but it was also much 'cleaner' in its exhaust emissions.

'Getting it in to the engine bay was quite a tight squeeze,' 'Folkson says, 'for though it was no longer than the T88, it was a lot more bulky. Getting the camshaft cover off the engine while it was in that bay was a bit of a performance!'

One consequence of the engine change was that the bulkhead needed to be modified so, as Richard told me with a grin: 'We needed a new heater, and so we also decided

to make the fascia look different! Along with central locking, electric windows and air conditioning as an option, this was a definite push up-market – and it would keep the Transit at the head of the sales charts for six more years.

'We did a lot of market research. Customer clinics and customer forums gave us lots of feedback – it was those which convinced us to provide more comfort, and more security. The programme was definitely "ad hoc" at first, then it just grew and grew – and therefore became VE83 ...

'In fact, giving programme approval for the VE83 was one of the first decisions our

From 1994, the latest Ford 2-litre 8-valve twin-overhead-camshaft petrol engine replaced the old single-cam 'Pinto' unit, which had been available on previous Transits since 1978.

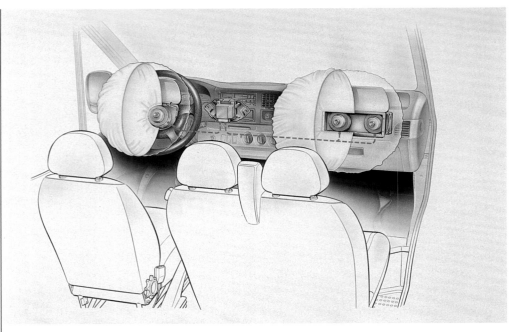

New legislation and market trends meant that the Transit VE83 of 1994 had twin airbags.

new top man, Jac Nasser, had to make. It came just one week after he had arrived in Europe.'

Even before then, the ebullient figure of Richard Parry-Jones had come back into this story, his enthusiasm lifting spirits of the Transit team once again. From 1992/93, as Chief Engineer, Ford-of-Europe, he had control of all new technical programmes.

Even though the Transit project was smaller than private-car schemes like the Mondeo, he still found time to visit Dunton and drive the vans.

'I used to go test driving – they were always very interesting and enjoyable days. Did I have better things to do with my time? Absolutely not, I had a portfolio of products, and had to allocate my time to cover all of

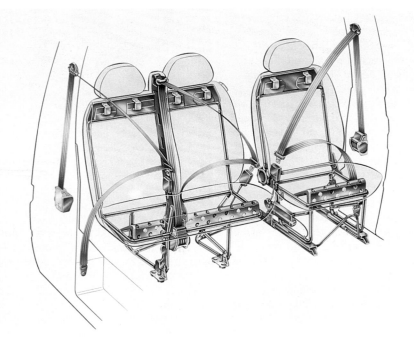

The clever feature of Transit safety belt engineering in the VE83 was that for the first time the centre passenger could also enjoy three-point shoulder harness protection.

them. But yes, I am extremely busy, so I don't have time to concentrate on Transit more than a few days every year ...

'Even so, I take the Transit responsibility very seriously, and always fitted in whatever time I could.'

Tongue in cheek, he then quipped: 'But *of course* I wanted to be involved. One was always aware that a disproportionate slice of the profits came from the Transit business! Whenever I had to run budget meetings, somehow or other that would come up. Even in Dearborn, at Ford-USA, the Transit registers often on their radar – because it makes good money, and of course a number of people back in Dearborn have previously spent a lot of time working in Europe, so they understand the thing ...'

The arrival of a fuel-injected twin-overhead-camshaft petrol engine made all the headlines, although safety changes including the use of airbags and full, three-point lap-and-diagonal seat belts for all three front passengers were never far behind.

A twin-cam engine on a Ford commercial vehicle – whatever next? In fact, this eight-valve 114bhp/2.0-litre power unit was already familiar in Ford's private cars – notably in Sierra and Granada/Scorpio models. It was the moment, too, when the venerable old 'Essex' V6 engine option was finally dropped.

It was the sign, in fact, of a general reshuffle and up-dating of Ford-of-Europe power units. The old 'Pinto' single-cam unit had been dropped from private cars in 1989, in favour of this Dagenham-built twin-cam, and now that the twin-cam had, in turn, been joined by the 16-valve 'Zetec' power unit in Escorts and Mondeos, it suddenly became available for Transit use.

Although such an engine was glamorous enough, in the Transit – and providing a lot more performance – in commercial terms it was still overshadowed, and outsold, by the valiant old 2.5-litre direct-injection diesel power unit. In fact, by the mid-1990s, very

A new Transit VE83 bus, being handed over to St Thomas's Hospital in 1998, by Chairman of Ford-of-Britain, Ian McAllister.

During the World Summit of 1999 in Cologne, Ford provided 100 LPG-powered Transit VE83s to transport thousands of media folk around.

Air conditioning in a Transit? Good grief – in the good old days, 'air conditioning' was provided by opening the windows …

Much attention had been given to safety features. Driver and passenger airbags were optional (the driver's bag, of course, was in the hub of the steering wheel), while three-point safety belts were now fitted to all three front seats. It had taken ages to engineer the installation for the centre seat, but spectacularly successful test results made it all worthwhile.

There was one more important novelty – the passenger-carrying executive bus varieties were now to be called 'Tourneo', rather than 'Transit', this being a name which soon became established as another Ford generic title. ('Tourneo'? The origins? No idea – this is another made-up Ford name, for my *Oxford English Dictionary* makes no mention.)

A six-year life

The VE83, being a new Transit derivative, deserved a good gimmick to set it off. British journalist Simon Harvey duly provided it, by driving a diesel-engined short-wheelbase Transit van, complete with a 500kg payload, on one complete lap of London's notorious M25 orbital motorway.

Observed by the Royal Automobile Club,

Transit minibuses have always been popular and successful models in the range.

Even when you are multi-millionaire pop stars, the Transit is still the best carry bag for all your gear. Slade collecting a new Transit from Ford-of-Britain's HQ at Brentwood in 1999.

few Transits were being sold with petrol power any more. For the VE83, the famous diesel was reworked yet again, this time to make it meet all proposed exhaust emission standards. It was now to be available in four different ratings – 70, 75, 85 and 100bhp.

The new interior must have impressed transport managers just as much, as Ford claimed that the new fascia was like that of the recently launched Mondeo passenger car; certainly, some features looked identical. Heating/ventilation had been revised, and full air conditioning became optional.

Simon completed this 120-mile plus lap non-stop, averaging a distinctly modest 50.02mph, but recording an amazing fuel consumption of more than 40mpg. This was no more than any commercial user would expect of such a well-proven vehicle.

It was almost a new beginning for a much-loved Ford success symbol, and before long, VE83s were in evidence everywhere. Pop groups (that ever-popular, but definitely earlier-generation Slade, was one of them) updated their fleets, while display teams needing 'kit buses' (such as the RAF Harrier support group) bought new examples.

Ford also found it easy to provide environmentally 'green' versions, converted to running on LPG, TV celebrity chef Gary Rhodes stowed most of his kit into one, while Britain's Royal Mail carried on using the vans as their main fleet model.

Late in the 1990s, Ford ran a stunningly effective TV advert for the Transit, dubbing it the 'Backbone of Britain', in which a long line of multi-hued Transits drove speedily across country, uphill and down dale, in close formation. Some cynics suggested that this was achieved by computer animation, but the pre-action still picture shown here proves otherwise.

Soon after VE83 went on sale, sales surged upwards. Not only were Southampton and Genk as busy as they had ever been, but an ever-expanding torrent of Transits were pouring out of the Turkish plant in Istanbul, and from 1996 to 2000 a limited number (about 2,500) were produced from CKD kits at Plonsk, in Poland.

Expansion in Turkey was steady, and extremely significant – for in 2004 a newly developed plant south-west of Istanbul would take Ford's prestige title as the 'lead plant' for all the Transit family. The very first Transits to be assembled in Turkey, all 300 of them, had been screwed together in 1967, the 5,000/year 'barrier' was breached

Transits have always been ideal machines to use for promotional purposes. Celebrity chef Gary Rhodes used this VE83 type for a nationwide tour in 1998.

In 1996, the RAF chose Transits for its support operation of the Harrier 'Jump Jet' display team.

Like many other courier companies, White Arrow relied heavily on Transit vans.

Ford mounted a stunningly effective British TV advert in 1999, showing scores of hard-working Transits trekking across country. Poised and ready to roll for the cameras, a VE83-type Royal Mail van leads at least thirty others, all of different, highly individual, shapes.

for the first time in 1975, nearly 10,000/year were being produced in the early 1990s, and once the VE83 had become available those figures were easily beaten.

Early Turkish-assembled Transits were kit built, but local manufacturing content (even of engines and chassis components) soon built up. At first these light trucks were for domestic sales, but exports eventually started, and by the 2000s this had become a vitally important operation indeed.

The figures produced in the appendices prove their point. In Turkey, 9,600 VE83s were built in 1995, 25,700 in 1996 and no fewer than 36,300 in 2000, when the change over to the new-generation Transit was about to take place.

Although there was a pending revolution in Transit style and layouts, behind the

scenes in the late 1990s, production and sales of the much-loved VE83 held up remarkably well. At Southampton, 77,000 were produced in 1998 – not quite an all-time record, but as many as the plant could manage (it was already being torn apart to make space for the next range) – while at Genk no fewer than 85,200 (which *was* an all-time record) were produced in the same year. Things looked good for the Transit – and there was more to come.

Transit in China

Although the Transit had already been built in no fewer than 22 different countries, the story of how Europe's favourite van came to be produced in China is fascinating. By the 1990s, although China remained a Communist state, it was allowing many more motor vehicles on to its roads, and its motor industry boomed as never before.

As a measure, in 1994, when Ford first took an interest in this vast nation, China was building only 250,000 cars and trucks in a year. Ten years later that had risen to nearly two million, and the trend lines were still sharply upwards.

At a time when the VE83 had just been launched, Ford-of-China's Norbert Kuhne approached his European colleagues: 'Why not come out to Shanghai, look around, and think about setting up Ford assembly facilities over here?'

Rod Hammonds and Eric Hoile therefore flew out to China, met top bosses from the Jiangling Motor Corporation (JMC) and set up a deal to build VE83 Transits out there. At the time, Jiangling were only building Isuzu pick-ups of rather ancient and unrefined heritage.

'We had to have 60 per cent local content,' Hoile told me, 'so we had to marry the VE83 to a four-cylinder Isuzu-based diesel engine, and use the locally manufactured five-speed Ford gearbox, with an Isuzu-based rear axle. Body pressings came out from Europe. That was in 1995, and eventually we launched the locally-built Transit in China in December 1997.'

At this time, Ford elected to carry on building VE83s in China even after 2000, when that model was discontinued in the rest of the world. Even today, in the mid-2000s, China-produced Transits are VE83-based. Assembly in a factory just one hour's drive from Shanghai, two hours from Beijing, began slowly – 2,220 were produced in 1997 – then built up inexorably. By 2003, when four-cylinder Mitsubishi-based petrol and Isuzu-based diesel derivatives were both available, JMC produced more than 11,000 Transits, and there was a lot more to come. Happily (I almost wrote 'naturally') by this time, the Transit was the best-selling European-sourced model in its class, in China. The principal 'take' in China was for buses, although vans and pick-ups were also in demand.

For Ford-of-China, was this just the start of something really big? If the success of a new model in Europe was any guide, it certainly looked like it. In 2000, as we are about to see, Ford had redefined the Transit, and what it was trying to do.

6 Front-wheel-drive, and an all-new Transit for 2000

By the early-1990s, Ford knew that the time had come to design an all-new Transit. The classic layout – front engine/rear-drive, with a long sweeping nose – had already been around for nearly a decade, and Ford's European rivals were beginning to announce really competitive products.

Rod Hammonds, at the time still directing the Transit engineering team, along with Mike Hallsworth, Nick Rochford and a handful of their colleagues, set up a tiny study group in October 1993 to work out what should be done to revive the brand in the future. At the same time, he was involved in work at Ford World HQ in Dearborn, USA to establish a rationalisation strategy.

'Basically,' Hammonds told me, 'we recommended that the commercial side of the European product business should be integrated in the commercial vehicle centre. This meant that future product development should move to North America – a very bold move.

'The resources and engineering capability in North America, particularly in computer-aided engineering (CAE) techniques, were much more advanced than anything we had in Europe.

'In fact, when we started asking around the engineering contract companies in the UK, for competitive bidding for projects, we found that the same-named individual (a specialist in his field) would figure in *all* their bids for CAE work!'

Mike Hallsworth (Vehicle Engineering Manager) spent a great deal of his time on forward-model concept consideration at this point: 'We started to talk to Hawtal Whiting, and it wasn't long before we decided that we needed two new vehicles, not one. Originally we were ahead of Product Planning on this, but we were always talking to them …'

Early discussions soon centred on the need for two separate projects, different in many ways, although if both had gone ahead it would have strained resources to the limit. Quite soon, it became clear that front-wheel-drive could be right for a 1-tonne van (smaller, shorter, with a low floor), while rear-wheel-drive was ideal for a 2-tonner.

'At that stage,' Mike recalled, 'the small project, a dedicated, front-wheel-drive van was coded VE104, the larger was the VE129, really a worked-over VE83.

We thought it made sense. The trouble was, that when Rod took these proposals to Jac Nasser, he showed them the door inside five minutes, saying that we couldn't afford two vehicles, so forget about it.'

From that moment, with top management adamantly against the idea of producing not one, but two new types of Transit, thoughts gradually began to turn to an all-can-do, almost infinitely flexible, single new platform. Here, the engines could be mounted in more than one position, and either front-wheel-drive or rear-wheel-drive could be accommodated. This had never before been attempted at Ford – nor had it been carried out by any of the rivals.

Richard Parry-Jones, no less, recalls that the Transit team was always sure that it could deliver the impossible: 'Were they arrogant? Yes. Maybe they were. They were very big-headed, very proud. They had achieved so much in previous models, that they knew – just knew – that they could do it again.'

'We knew we needed a new petrol engine,' Folkson says, 'because of the way emissions laws were changing, and we needed an all-new family of diesel engines. We had always bought lots of competitive vehicles, to see what our rivals had to offer. We tested them, ran them round our durability courses, stripped them, and even crash tested them.'

By 1993/94 – even before the last of the traditional Transits, the VE83, was unveiled, concept work for a new model was well under way.

'I attended packaging meetings at Dunton,' Graham Symonds told me, 'with my boss, Andy Jacobson. At the time, a new Transit product, only a front-wheel-drive machine at that stage, was being shaped and designed at Dunton, but the engineering and packaging was being done for Ford, but outside the company, at Hawtal Whiting. This much respected contract engineering business was based in Basildon, and was employing several one-time senior ex-Ford personalities.

'In fact, I was totally against what Dunton Design was doing – even though they had spent a good deal of money – because their solution was an extreme "fast front" almost like a train. This had been influenced by the American Vice President running the programme at the time.

'But it was walking away from our market, because the driver was positioned too low. When we sat in the mock-up, we

The new-generation V184/V185 Transit range was conceived in the USA. By 1998, and even before the programme returned to Dunton in Essex, the Transit team was sizeable, and a fleet of lightly disguised prototypes already existed. Public launch would follow in 2000.

Big Boys'
toys ...

To modify a remark about new-vehicle engineering, once made to me by the legendary technical chief of Jaguar, William Heynes: 'Pencil and paper is cheap, but cutting metal is expensive ...'

Nowadays, of course, we would substitute 'computers' for 'pencil and paper', but the aphorism still applies, which explains why, way back in the 1990s, when a new-generation Transit was being talked about, all manner of features were discussed, even if not turned into real engineering.

As options, for instance, what would you think of self-levelling, or even 'kneeling' suspension? Of adaptive suspension damping? Of four-wheel-drive? Of a sun-roof option for bus derivatives? Of further engine transplants?

Technically, of course, the ability to develop all such fittings exists. But, on a Transit? Who knows ...

By the time the V184/V185 generation of Transits was launched in 2000, the Southampton plant had been expanded to the limit of its boundaries. The grey block in the centre of this view covered the ultra-modern paint shop. Yes, the factory really is that close to Southampton Airport.

couldn't envisage why it was the way it was. My opinion was that we had to have the driver sitting up in a traditional Transit position, and modernise the vehicle – and, by the way, at that time I thought we should stay with rear-wheel-drive, we shouldn't go for front-wheel-drive. I nearly lost my job for saying that!'

At that time, as Symonds recalls, he and Ford-USA were almost on a collision course with the Dunton approach, and that he was often challenged for authorising an alternative style. Like others at Ford, he was convinced that his team's more traditional style, with the ability to position a high load floor (rear-wheel-drive) or low floor (front-wheel-drive) was the way to go.

Symonds, whose Transit design team was centred at Dearborn, also recalls sending a team to the Genk plant, to ask about limitations: 'The feedback we got from the Belgians was that body length wasn't a big problem, increased width would be a terrible problem, and height could also be a problem. The amount of investment we were able to save, by not making the production engineers rip up everything, was colossal.'

Barry Gale (Chief Programme Engineer in

the mid-2000s), told me that: 'Many customers wanted a low floor, but to do that we had to move the big rear axle out of the way. The low-floor is 4.0in [100mm] lower than the rear-wheel-drive type – and that's a big gain.'

By this time thinking behind the new project had moved on, with VE104 and VE129 *both* replaced by VE160, which was to be transverse-engined, all front-wheel-drive except for the heavy-duty chassis-cab, which would need rear-wheel-drive and twin rear wheels.

Mike Hallsworth commented: 'We knew the chassis-cabs had to have twin rear wheels to carry the loads – and they had to be driven rear wheels in order to get traction. Somehow or other we had to drive those rear wheels – Rod Hammonds and myself hated to have to admit this, but we carried out a series of load, gradability tests and proved the point at the top end of the range.

'We were stuck with having to find a way of driving those rear wheels. We lumbered the transmission people with finding a way of power to the rear wheels for that particular version – and they couldn't find a valid solution.'

In the meantime, by mid-1994, the Transit team had learned of the launch of Ford 2000, and had become convinced that they needed to move to Dearborn to do their job. Alex Trotman's strategy was taking place, which recognised that Ford was now a complex world-wide business, selling its products all over the world, yet it was still designing, developing and marketing too many different products. Ford 2000 set out to globalise the business by allocating new product development and leadership to five centres, with Truck Development settling at Dearborn.

In effect, Ford-of-Europe was to control the future of light and medium cars, while Ford-USA was to control the Large Car Group, the Speciality Car Group, the Light Truck Group and the Commercial Truck Group. The most sensible place, it seemed to the Dunton-based Transit team, was that they should be fitted into the Commercial Truck Group. Accordingly, they lobbied for the engineering of the new model to be centred on Dearborn, where the expertise was high, and the resources impressive.

'Right from the start,' Mike Hallsworth told me, 'we said we had to go to the States

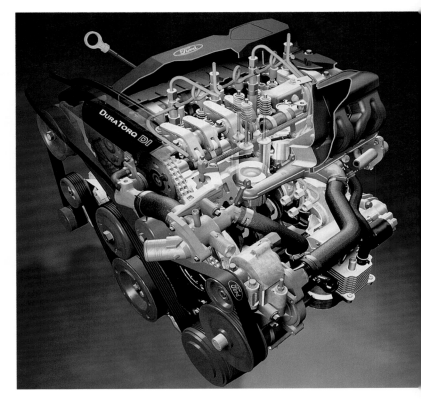

Ford developed a brand-new 16-valve diesel engine, eventually with 'common-rail' technology, for use in the V184/V185 Transit range from 2000. It could be installed transversely (for front-wheel-drive) or in-line (for rear-wheel-drive). This was such an excellent engine it was also adopted for use in the latest Mondeo passenger car – and even in the Jaguar X-type!

The fascia/instrument panel/steering wheel of the V184/V185 Transit was very car-like in every way.

to do the job, and eventually management believed us.'

Rod Hammonds was also sure that this was right: 'I don't think I could have got such a massive programme approved – massive in terms of workload and finance – sitting in a European environment, without daily contact with my North American colleagues.'

Without doubt, this was the highest investment in a European commercial vehicle programme that Ford had ever made.

(But it wasn't always easy. There was even a frivolous suggestion that Ford should buy an old aircraft carrier, moor it in mid-Atlantic, use the flight deck for testing, and do all the work away from national influences. When the time came to launch, it was suggested, the carrier could then be brought back to Europe ...)

Once the decision to go to the USA had been ratified, before the end of 1994 a series of drive appraisals were held in Europe, where current Transits were compared with their competitors. These were based in the Ardennes, not far from the test track at Lommel, and took place at the end of 1994. This gave newly appointed staff from the

USA the opportunity to sample the Transit and European driving conditions, for the very first time.

'The debrief after the final drive appraisal,' Hallsworth told me, 'was most significant. The final pre-announcement VE6 management drive review had been held, way back in 1985, just before the old team was dispersed, with a debrief in the same hotel in Eindhoven, talking things through in the same conference room as now. It was almost like seeing a Phoenix reborn!'

At this juncture, Hawtal Whiting made a series of presentations to Ford-USA management (including Dave Grandinett), therefore initiating a tidy handover process from Essex to Dearborn. Hawtal Whiting, which had a large operation based in the USA, and run by former VE6 engineer David Jones, was looking forward to keeping a major involvement with this project.

This, though, was not to be, for by this time Ford-USA had decided not to 'out-source' such a major programme, and Hawtal Whiting was finally released in the first half of 1995. Ford required new thinking this time around, for it was felt that Hawtal Whiting (which employed many ex-

Ford personalities who had already been involved in the VE6 and other Transit derivatives) represented Transit's past, not its future.

Thus, the future of the Transit came to lean heavily on Ford patronage in the USA. Accordingly, in 1995, when a definite start was made on an all-new Transit, work began in Dearborn, under the leadership of the American Dave Grandinett. Dave arrived, carrying a huge amount of Ford-USA 'light truck' experience, including working on the original Explorer of the early 1990s, and on the very successful Windstar project.

Dave, always involved on the VE160 project became Chief Programme Engineer, once the intention of moving the operation to Dearborn had been agreed, and would head up much of the nagging which led to agreement to develop two separate mechanical layouts. He would control the project until 2000, when the new model finally began to roll down three assembly lines in Europe.

'We had to sit down for a long time,' Dave says, 'to ask ourselves a load of strategic questions – how big, how many different types, which end the drive should be? All that sort of stuff. Not everyone was agreed. We assumed nothing.'

'Without him,' Richard Folkson (who succeeded Nick Rochford in 1994) insists, 'back in Europe, I think we would have carried on with two different projects, trying to find ways of producing two separate platforms. Maybe we would even have ended up with a car-derived front-wheel-drive solution. He saw that the engine, as a whole, was very square – as wide as it is long.

'Even so, although we used computers to help us with layouts, we struggled with this for months – the critical problem being that if we adopted an in-line engine as well, we wanted to keep a common steering rack/steering column position ...'

The original conundrum was that if the rack was correctly positioned for the transverse engine installation, it would foul the engine/transmission in its in-line engine installation. In the end, and after a lot of pushing, pulling, raising and lowering, the 'north-south' [in line] engine had to be moved to let that rack slot into place.'

Even before then, of course, the concept was purely of a front-wheel-drive machine, the very first that Ford had ever attempted

The medium-wheelbase, high-roof V184 Transit, with rear-wheel-drive, is one of the stalwarts of the new-for-2000 range. It was only one of many different derivatives.

on a large van. Technically elegant though it was (private car engineers already knew this!), the principal advantage was that without a propeller shaft, a very low loading floor (4in/100mm lower than before) could be provided. Because the competition – from VW and Renault in particular – had already gone down that road, the possibilities needed to be explored.

'Well before we moved to Dearborn,' Hallsworth remembers, 'we built a couple of front-wheel-drive "mules". We didn't need disguise – we based one of them on a VW T4 van, and another on a Fiat Ducato!'

On this basis a British team, which totalled 35–40 people at first (but it never increased beyond this figure), moved to the USA, into buildings close to the massive Ford Proving Ground and Engineering Centre in Dearborn. There they carried on working on the VE160, as it was then known, and stayed for nearly four years.

This team largely took over an in-house

organisation which had originally been working on the Ford-USA 'Helios' programme, which was to produce a small passenger car to rival the Chrysler Neon. This team, which had used a lot of CAE, had found the 'Helios' project cancelled in mid-1994. Eventually, at least 500–600 ambitious people became available, were appointed, and began to swarm all over the burgeoning Transit project before the end of the year.

'There were American Ford people over there,' Trevor Mills reminded me, 'who were kicking their heels, and this was an ideal way to get them involved again.'

As Dave Grandinett also quipped: 'We had a lot of young people on board, too, who hadn't been involved in trucks before, and didn't know you couldn't do certain things. Very refreshing!'

European expertise and experience was certainly needed to make sure that a new Transit did not become an American vehicle. Ford-USA was already building the very

Ford's largest-ever investment in a commercial vehicle produced the Transit with front- or rear-wheel-drive. Once delivered, not many stayed as clean as this for long!

Opposite This 2000 Ford publicity shot emphasised that the Transit could work around the clock. Moody stuff, right?

Front-wheel-drive, or rear-wheel-drive

It would take a complete book to describe every twist-and-turn in the evolution of the new-generation Transits which finally appeared in 2000. First thoughts went into developing a new front-wheel-drive model, then into a separate, larger, rear-drive model to go with it, after which it was proposed that both should be launched at the same time.

Top management having killed that scheme, the engineers then favoured the front-wheel-drive solution, although once direction came from Dearborn, it was suggested that rear-wheel-drive, on its own, should be chosen instead.

Eventually, and after a lot of deep thinking, and much work in CAE (computer-aided engineering) systems, the idea of developing both layouts in the same basic structure took shape – and was eventually approved. In the end, the only downside to this was that new rear-drive Transits went on sale six months before the front-wheel-drive variety was ready.

In the 2000s, as in the 1960s, a high proportion of all Transits were delivered as chassis-cab types, so that customers could have their own special rear bodies fitted.

Transits don't come much bigger than this! On the longest wheelbase, with the 'Jumbo' chassis extension, this 17-seater bus was an example of just how large the new V185 type could become.

successful Econoline which, although it had a similar 'cube', was not at all the sort of van the Europeans wanted to copy – if only because it had vast V8 engines, for in the USA, operating economy was still not an issue! Although the Econoline is, itself, an icon in North America, it is a much simpler, very basic, machine, but in terms of payload, package and power-train efficiency it is a very different, even outdated, product, and Transit had little to learn from it.

Even so, there was a healthy 'truck' atmosphere, a mass of North American commercial vehicle know-how, and the knowledge that Ford-USA was the most successful concern in that market sector – all of which made Dearborn a very fertile place in which to start developing a new design.

In the meantime, the style/design of the new Transits took shape, first in Dunton, and later in Dearborn. At one point, Ford's advanced design studio in California produced a sensational offering, but this was way 'out of package', and only elements of it could be used in the final chosen shape. At that stage, Graham Symonds was the only Briton with any influence, and he already had much Dearborn experience with F-Type and Ranger trucks:

'Our team also included two Koreans, a Romanian, and an Egyptian as well as resident Americans.'

It was an experienced, multi-talented, multi-national design team – and the result was impressive. More angular than the VE83 which it would replace, but ingeniously detailed so that the combination of wheelbase lengths and body heights could all be accommodated in one complex set of press tooling, it would be instantly recognisable, different from the old model, but still recognisably a Transit. Although it looked slightly more angular than before, the drag coefficient had actually been massaged slightly downwards – so operating economy and fuel consumption were not likely to be affected.

To the author, not a styling expert, the most praiseworthy aspects were the complex new dash/fascia/instrument package – which was designed to be installed, from the side (with the body shell doors still removed) on the assembly lines, the way that normal-

height or low-loading floors were so logically welded to the rest of the structure as required, and the smart way in which the glass was applied to the Tourneo/bus derivatives.

Two layouts

The big news in 2000, was that the all-new Transit would be produced in two entirely different forms – VE185 with front-wheel-drive, or VE184 with rear-wheel-drive. Not only that, but front-wheel-drive types had a transversely mounted engine/transmission, while rear-drive types had the conventional in-line engine/transmission/propeller shaft system. At a casual glance, the front-wheel-drive engine/transmission looked as if might have come straight out of a Mondeo diesel – but although there were some common components, the reality, in detail, was rather different, and the Transit team insists that *they* were first! Certainly the investment costs quoted at that stage were enormous.

Even so, the argument over layouts had intensified soon after the Transit operation in Dearborn had opened up. Chairman Alex Trotman, no less, had his doubts, and back in Europe the marketing staffs were having second thoughts about using front-wheel-drive with larger payloads, although they insisted that a low load floor was also essential.

It would be fair to say that many North American personalities were originally dead set against a front-wheel-drive layout – and were only convinced after the new 'twins' began to sell so well in the 2000s. Ken Dabrowski, the Vice-President running this programme, was a rear-wheel-drive fan, but

agreed that data – facts, not suppositions – should decide. For some months in 1995, however, he was vocally against choosing front-wheel-drive at all, wanting traditional rear-wheel-drive instead.

Such a battle, of course, was going to affect the definitive layout of the new family of 'Puma' diesel engines currently being finalised, for the location of engine-driven accessories for a transversely mounted engine was sure to be very different from that of in-line mounted power units.

'As a result of this,' Hallsworth reminded me, 'we had to carve up some of our early prototype engines – which were all laid out for front-wheel-drive machines – and convert them into rear-wheel-drive engines instead!'

Months later, and after many spirited

It isn't always glamorous. In the early 2000s, M-Sport used a fleet of different trucks and vans, including new-generation Transits, in their support of the 'works' Ford Focus WRC rally cars.

Design of the modern-generation Transit was completed in the USA in 1995/96. This was an early clay-model development of the new vehicle.

discussions, the Transit team solved the dilemma in an ingenious manner. Instead of designing one or the other – they would evolve *both* types. Not only that, but they would ensure that the two installations shared the same structure, the same engine bay, independent front suspension and power-assisted steering.

'The real breakthrough', Hammonds told me, 'was when the engineers found a way of

retaining 95 per cent commonality, and using a common platform.

'But for a time I had grave doubts that this could be achieved, and concentrated on a front-wheel-drive layout at first. But from the data, it was clear that there was a cross-over point at about 1.5 tonnes payload, for above that there were benefits from having rear-wheel-drive. I believe we were the first company to achieve front-wheel-drive *and*

In 1998, Ford showed off a Transit Concept to gauge reaction. At that stage, though, a different type of nose was fitted.

At the design stage in 1995/96, a full-size clay model of the V184/V185 series was put outside for a management viewing.

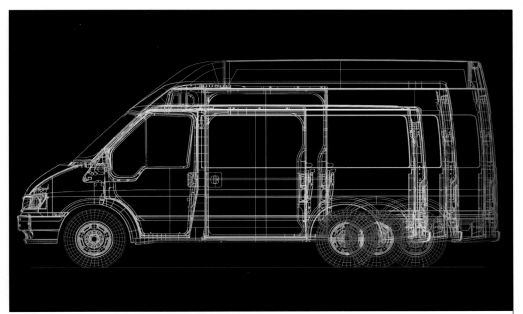

From the very beginning, the 2000-generation Transit was always set to be built with three wheelbases, and three different body heights. This wire frame study shows how it was achieved.

rear-wheel-drive in the same basic vehicle.'

When the time came to launch the new vehicle to the press, Ford proved its point in a remarkable way, as Hallsworth recalled: 'It is possible to convert a Transit from a running "north-south" engine, with rear-wheel-drive, to a running "east-west" engine, with front wheel drive, in just 20 minutes!'

Difficulties in laying out both engine/transmission assemblies – to fit the same body structure, and to keep a common steering rack/front suspension design – went on for so long that Grandinett feared they were running out of time.

'He pushed us to have a closed-door session,' Folkson remembers with a smile, 'more or less telling us that we weren't going to be let out until had solved everything. It was in a little side office unit at Dearborn. Once we found a common solution for the steering rack, everything else fell into place ...

'Manufacturing, who would have to build two very different types of Transit down the same assembly line, back-to-back, were also involved ...'

'Then we had to convince our top colleagues in Dearborn, who still thought that *all* trucks should be designed like their own Econoline. The *real* breakthrough was when we convinced them that we should be allowed to go ahead ...'

Mike Hallsworth confirmed all this, noting that it came to a climax, and a solution was found, in mid-1995. Using the same body shell, which would only have to be lightly modified for a particular installation, the team elected to offer both types. From outside the new-generation Transit, it would be almost impossible to spot which was which – the easy clue being to look under the rear of the chassis to see if there was a driven axle, or merely a beam! It was such an ingenious solution that Ford

The 2000MY Transit was the first to use a conventional MacPherson strut independent front suspension system. Very cleverly, this was made compatible with front-wheel-drive or rear-wheel-drive installations.

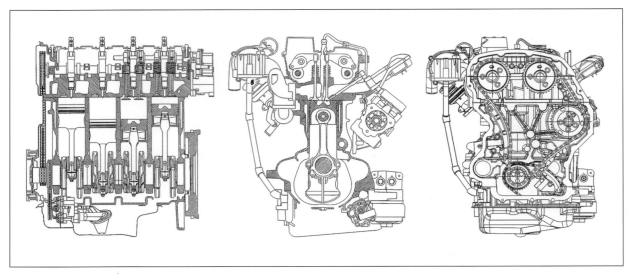

These drawings of the Duratorq diesel confirm the neat twin overhead camshaft/16-valve cylinder head layout.

By any standards, the 2000-generation Transit had the most complex fascia/instrument panel yet used in this model line. The entire pre-assembled structure was fed in to the body shell, by robot handling, through a door aperture.

was sure that, one day, its rivals would copy them, but five years later, there was no sign of this.

Not only that, but Ford's determination to provide three wheelbase lengths and three heights – and almost every possible combination of the two – was enormously demanding in terms of manufacturing facilities. Ford is still proud of the fact that none of its rivals has yet matched the sheer choice made available.

'It was a real technical challenge,' Grandinett admitted, 'but we managed it! Was there ever a time when we were threatened with having to cancel one or other of the layouts? Yes – absolutely. Whether or not we could actually deliver

two layouts was always a question, and whether we could do it within the limits of allocated investment was beyond our experience.

'I had to sell the two-layout chassis to my superiors very regularly – again and again. I reckon it took years off my life – but we made it. We were not about to give up, and we were not about to fail!'

This proved several things – not only that the engineers were amazingly resourceful, and that designers/stylists could wrap the same shape around a multitude of engines, but that a modern four-cylinder engine assembly was almost as wide as it was long. If you don't believe that then have a look at the engine fitted in your own vehicle, and

realise how much the fuel injection, the manifolding, and the mass of pumps and alternators all add to the width.

Apart from this, the truly brave decision was to engineer a new Transit layout, and a brand-new family of diesel engines at the same time. This happens rarely – especially in a multi-national company like Ford. It is more usual to introduce a new engine on an existing model, or to start a new model on existing engines before phasing in a new power unit two or three years later.

Because of Ford's decision to go for this revolutionary choice of engine positions for the new Transit (and although it might not look like it, packaging constraints were very tight), and because of the need to produce a powerful, fuel-efficient, low-emissions power unit, there was really no choice. Even before the V184/V185 projects took wings, the design of a new 'Puma' diesel engine (later officially titled 'Duratorq') was under way.

'Although it wasn't our responsibility,' Hallsworth insists, 'we had a lot of influence on it. Our main input, again and again, was to insist that it had to be a real truck engine, with all the reliability and durability that was so typical of the Transit.'

Engineered and developed at Dunton in Essex, the 16-valve, twin-cam, four-cylinder 'Puma' was an enormously ambitious project. Relatively conventional at first, it might once have used balancer shafts to make it ultra-smooth (provision is still there, in the cylinder block, for those shafts to be inserted), and inherited 'common-rail'

injection technology from 2002 onwards. It took shape as an ultra-modern diesel intended for use in trucks *and* cars, so a modern factory complex and new facilities were needed at Dagenham.

For this, the company announced a $1 billion (£600 million) programme in 1997, for a brand-new diesel engine, this being one of three major investments in new diesel engines (with the 1.75-litre 'common-rail' diesel for the Transit Connect and the passenger-car 2.7-litre V6 of 2004) being made in this period.

Along the way, the Transit team had originally planned to have a 2.4-litre engine for transverse mounting. In the 1994/95 period, when V. P. Dabrowski insisted on an

Somewhere in there is an engine! Ford was so confident that its Transit engines would need little service and maintenance, that it made the engine bay extremely compact.

Life as a development engineer is not always glamorous. New-generation Transits were tested, rigorously, in these Arctic conditions in Canada, in the late 1990s.

A line of new-generation Transits, along with an old-type VE83 model, pausing during a hot-weather test session in Arizona. The three new models carried front-end disguise.

Five new-model Transits on test in Arizona in the late 1990s. All carried disguise, not unlike that of the existing VE83 model. The second in line, hidden by development staff, actually is a VE83, which was being used for comparator duties.

in-line/rear-drive installation, they then had to return to the Power Train people, asking for rather different 2.4-litre versions to be engineered for in-line usage.

When the decision was then made to offer both installations, a further approach was made to Power Train, who replied that this time it was *not* going to be possible – but they could supply 2.0-litre 'Pumas' instead! This provided extra headaches for all the engineers and, unavoidably, delayed the transverse-engine programme by between six and twelve months.

Well before it was ready for the Transit, in fact, the 2.0-litre 'Puma' was already being finalised for use in the new-generation Mondeo passenger car. By 2003, too, it would be available in the Jaguar X-type (whose platform was based on that of the Mondeo), and had built a fine reputation. In

many ways, though, 'Puma' had a much-discussed birth.

'At first there were enormous debates about the engine capacity,' Folkson told me, 'Should it be 2.0 litres, 2.5 litres, 2.2 litres, or 2.4 litres? Which size, in which derivative, what power and torque – we were involved right the way from the start.'

'We kidded the engine people along, for a long time,' Hallsworth confirms, 'that we wanted an "east-west" 2.4-litre engine, instead of the 2.0-litre we eventually settled for. And then we asked them to provide a "north-south" 2.4 instead! That meant relocating all the auxiliaries …'

While all this was going on, the Transit team also had to make provision for a petrol engine alternative. Even though the take-up of petrol engines is now very small (less than three per cent of all orders these days, and

on a recent day-long visit to Southampton I did not see a single petrol-powered machine …) there was still a small but definite demand. In some cases, these are users of luxury courtesy buses, and in others, Transit owners operating in heavily polluted cities where diesel engines are banned, need it.

'The most significant examples in the early 2000s,' Barry Gale informed me, 'are LPG users, Athens, Mexico, congestion-charge cities and so on …'

In earlier submissions (VE160) the proposed petrol engine was a 2.3-litre 8-valve twin-cam derived from the old-style 1994–2000 Transit 2.0-litre line up, and due to be rated at 130bhp. Before long, however, it became clear that this engine would soon be withdrawn from the line-up, and that the 16-valve derivative (as used in cars as diverse as the Escort RS2000, the Galaxie MPV and the Scorpio private cars) could be used instead. This was the very first time, therefore, that high-tech four-valve engine technology was to be used, right across the board, in the Transit.

'In any case,' Folkson quipped, 'you need 16-valve breathing to help meet modern emissions requirements …'

With no bulky axle casing to accommodate underneath, front-wheel-drive allowed Ford to provide a very low load floor on the 2000-generation Transit.

By the 2000s, ice-cream vans and the Transit brand had been together for well over 30 years.

This aggressive-looking cactus plant in an Arizona desert reminds the crew that the sun is up there, and that their air-conditioning installation has to work well!

I never thought I would find a pile of rocks visually stunning, but judge for yourself … this rear-drive V185 was built in 2001.

All this, of course, had to be linked in with modern transmissions. Rear-drive Transits used up-dated MT75 five-speeders (also from 1990s Transits), while front-wheel-drive types used VXT75 five-speeders (which were related to those used in Mondeos and Galaxy MPVs, but more durable, being built up to Transit engineers' rigorous requirements).

For the first time, however, there was to be no conventional automatic transmission, although a clutchless 'stick-shift' alternative called 'Durashift' was available on rear-drive versions.

As ever, much horse-trading went on between engineering, product-planning and the cost accountants. It helps, of course, to be part of a massive, multi-national, organisation, where there may be several alternatives.

As an example, early in the development of the new machine at Dearborn, the team was looking for a small-diameter steering

Production
– five million
and more

Ford was so busy moving Transit assembly from Genk (Belgium) to Kocaeli (Turkey) in 2003/04 that the five-millionth Transit slipped through without a fanfare. In fact, there was no need for any further celebrations, as the Transit brand is now a best-selling European light/medium commercial vehicle by any measure.

A quick skim of the detailed figures provided by Ford shows that production (and demand, of course) continues to rise, limited only by available factory space. For some time the record was held by the 1989 calendar year when nearly 178,000 Transits were produced in four plants – Azambuja, Genk, Istanbul and Southampton – but more than 200,000 were assembled for the first time in 2000, when the all-new V184/V185 models came on stream.

Even so, the arrival of the Connect, this making the Transit into a family of two ranges, saw new records being broken with ease. In 2003, the first full year of Connect production, no fewer than 264,300 Transits of all types were built on five sites. The next hurdle, of building more than 300,000 in 12 months, must surely be breached in the years to come.

In 2004, the records kept on rolling. The 100,000th Connect was assembled early in the year – and the quarter millionth will follow by mid-2005. By 2005 the 500,000th Turkish-assembled 'full-size' Transit is due to be built – and this is only the beginning.

A study in profiles – both are 2001-built rear-wheel-drive Transits.

wheel, found that the Ford Ranger wheel was ideal *and* that it delivered a $10 saving per unit.

'One reason,' Trevor Mills recalls, 'was that Ford was already making 1.5 million of those wheels every year. An extra 200,000 wasn't going to frighten the supplier all that much!'

The chosen fascia layout, too, was brand-new for the Transit, but an earlier version of it had already been developed by design as one offering in the new-generation Ford-USA F150 truck. After an alternative had been chosen for the F150, this excellent assembly then became available for the Transit.

'When we developed it,' Gale told me, 'we had a stock of maps, clip-boards, cups, cans and Thermos flasks to try out – because we'd asked people what they carried, and observed what, and where, they carried them. We allowed for cup holders too.

'We included a mobile phone holder too – and now the legislation has changed in the UK, so fewer people are actually using them on the move in Transits …'

Even though great strides were made in standardising the two layouts, in effect there were still two new models, with a six-month gap in progress between the two types. In the end, V184 (rear drive) was ready first, but V185 (FWD) had to follow on more than half a year behind.

Once prototype vehicle testing started, the new Transits were sent to many different locations in North America. Some work was carried out at the Romeo Proving Ground – which is about 50 miles north of Detroit – before hot-climate work began in another Ford proving ground in Arizona, while winter work was carried out a long way north, in Canada. Much of the rough-road durability work, incidentally, was carried out back in Europe, at Lommel, in Belgium.

During that period, between 100 and 150 prototypes – some of them incomplete vehicles – were built in North America, and several were hurled into crash barriers as part of the legislative work needed to gain approval all around the world. That number would double before the production lines began to turn out new-generation Transits in earnest.

Well before 'pilot build' could begin at Genk, Ford decided to construct a further group of 25 disguised prototypes (at the front, they looked rather like Ford-USA Econolines), which would then be loaned out to well-respected customers, and put to work in Britain, Germany and Turkey. The first went into service in May 1999. Such programmes already existed, but using existing models with development changes installed – this, though, was the first time the customers had got their hands on a model before it officially existed.

Before the new model was ready to be put on sale, the Ford 2000 initiative had been

The transversely mounted 'common-rail' diesel engine was introduced to the Transit in 2002. Amazingly, that engine bay can (and does) also accommodate in-line ('north-south') engines too, without modification.

Just one of the many
different 2000s-Transit
styles – this being the
base front-wheel-drive
van, with high roof line.

severely modified, so much so that Ford-of-Europe (under Nick Scheele) once again became important, and the Transit programme (as one of that company's jewels) was speedily swept back into Europe. Any thought of putting the new Transit on the market in the USA always had to consider the huge extra burden of legislative, testing and compliance work which would be needed, and little was ever done to make that possible. One day, though, maybe one day …

Engineers began to come back from the USA in 1999, to live with the developing launch of the two new trucks in Europe. Mike Hallsworth took that opportunity to retire, the Transit being the last major project on his Ford CV, and Rod Hammonds soon followed him. Within months, offices and workshops in Dearborn, which had been heaving with Transit work, became deserted, fell silent and were soon abandoned. Those who came home to the UK were just in time to see the arrival of a pivotal new product.

On sale

By comparison with the eventful development period, launch and production of the new model was positively conventional. As planned some years earlier, Ford was ready to launch the new-generation Transit in January 2000, immediately after it had celebrated the arrival of the four millionth machine of all, and first deliveries were made in March 2000.

Although front-wheel-drive and rear-wheel-drive types were both previewed together, it was the rear-drive types which went on sale first, with front-drive types following in the autumn of the same year.

When I began writing this book, Chief Programme Engineer Barry Gale confused me utterly by demonstrating just how many different types of new Transit had become available. Apart from three wheelbases, three roof heights and four lengths (including the lengthy 'Jumbo' model in which SVO had been much involved), there were several ratings of diesel engine and the 16-valve petrol engine, and he pointed out that the 'cubes' took account of standard builders' material dimensions, car park height restrictions and the dimensions of a Euro pallet!

Much of the investment in this new model went into laying down facilities – not only for the Duratorq diesel engine at Dagenham, but also at the major assembly plants. Hundreds of millions went into Genk, Southampton, and a new factory at Kocaeli in Turkey – more than £200 million into Southampton alone.

One quirk of modernisation at Southampton was that the factory could no longer spread sideways, for it had reached the limits of its property. Nor can it even spread far upwards as this would interfere with the flight-path of the nearby Southampton Airport. Inserting a new paint shop, therefore, was a very ticklish, but remarkably successful, operation.

Who should make what, and where? This was a conundrum, in which factory layouts, and future policy all had an influence. Because Southampton was over-full, and cramped in some places, the longest wheelbase version could not be built there. All and every type could be – and were – built at Genk. It was from, this point, that the new factory at Kocaeli, came into the reckoning.

Described more fully in Chapter 8, this plant was originally scheduled to make only the new 'little brother', Transit Connect. In the 2000s, however, Ford's new policy of allocating 'Lead Plant' status to each model range saw Genk take control of Mondeo and related machinery, while Kocaeli was rapidly expanded, to become 'Lead Plant' for *both* the Transits. From 2004, in fact, Transit assembly would end at Genk, 39 years after it had begun.

But, after all the heartache of development, would the new twin-models sell? Although there was the set-back at Kocaeli caused by the earthquake, the arrival of the new model *and* a gradual move to the new factory didn't help, but the Turkish plant pushed ahead in 2002 and 2003, while in all the sales indicators pointed upwards.

Statisticians had to sift carefully through the 2000 figures, as the old model was still being built until mid-year. This was also the year in which no fewer than five Transit VE83 (old-model) satellite plants (in Belarus, Malaysia, Poland, Portugal and Vietnam) closed down reducing the number of

Product placement, British Telecom style, with one of that company's huge fleet of Transits posed on London's Westminster Bridge. 'Big Ben' is in the background. Not much traffic, though – so it has to be a Sunday afternoon, surely?

locations where Transits were assembled to only four.

Even so, within months Ford knew that they had got it right. Genk, it seemed, was determined to make its point before it lost its status as the Transit's 'Lead Plant'. After building 74,500 in 1999, it produced 90,700 in 2000 (model changeover year), and an all-time record of 100,000 in 2001, with 94,400 following on in 2002.

This was also a time when SVO began another vigorous push – to win back some business from specialised areas, notably in the motor caravan trade.

'Transit volume is building up again,' Angus Macleod says, 'because we can now make the "base vehicle" much more suitable for caravan conversions, with different suspension and other items, with back cab panel cut-outs, do roof cut-outs with reinforcements in other places to keep within seat-belt strength legislation, and so on. The low floor on the front-wheel-drive Transit helps a lot, too.'

Although the new-generation Transit was crowned with the International Van of the Year award in 2001, there was no time for

complacency. Where to make vans, and how to make more of them, was always a problem. Even though no attempt had ever been made to sell the Transit in the USA, it was being sold in 55 other territories.

In Britain, there was no doubt that the public liked what it saw. While 49,858 of the old-model (VE83) Transit had been sold in 1999, 54,167 of the new-generation machine were sold in 2001, and that rose to 57,214 in 2003. By that time, effectively, at home the restriction was on the ability to produce, rather than sell, the product.

The problem was that, in spite of all the investments made over the years, Southampton was overcrowded. Amazingly, 25 Transits an hour – up to a theoretical maximum of 375 vans a day – could be built, but there was enough demand for that to be increased if there had been more space. From 2003, Genk began to be run down as Kocaeli was built up.

Although no styling changes were made, improvements and additions to the range came steadily in the next few years. In April 2002 the first new-generation 17-seater bus derivatives were launched: 'Now the

Transits have always made successful VIP airport buses.

Transit can be chauffeur-driven,' Barry Gale quipped, 'and take a complete rugby team ...'

Next, in summer, was the arrival of the advanced, high-tech 'common-rail' diesel engines on which Ford had been working for so long, and then in mid-2003 ABS anti-lock braking (already optional since launch) was standardised.

More technical advance was on the way. In April 2004, not only did Ford up-grade the rear-drive 2.4-litre diesel engine to 135bhp, but linked it with a newly developed six-speed manual transmission. Not only was this the most powerful diesel engine yet fitted to a Transit, but it was also the first time six-speeds had been seen. That new transmission, incidentally, was not related to the six-speeder we also saw in the latest diesel-engined Jaguar S-type, announced only a few weeks away.

The latest engines, incidentally, gave the Transit the sort of performance which could only have been dreamed of in early days. With the 135bhp diesel, Ford claimed a 98mph top speed, so in the rare case of the petrol-powered 16-valve being unleashed, this might have been the first-ever Transit to reach a genuine 100mph.

But that was not all – and never likely to be all. Even as this book was first published, Ford had many new Transit projects under development – facelifts, derivatives, more

SVO action (especially in transmissions) and additional marketing wheezes – so I doubt if there will be a 'complete story' for many years to come. At the same time, it was on its way to becoming a 'world' product.

Global engineering boss Richard Parry-Jones gleefully reminded me that although the Transit had always been European-based, it was rapidly building up a market in China, and that other territories were due to be assaulted in the future. So why not in America?

'Transit was always designed to operate in Europe, where the roads were congested. In the States, the space problem is not as serious, so Ford-USA's own trucks were larger, and more expansive, to suit. But I believe that one day – one day – Transit's day will come in North America. The latest 'common-rail' diesels are so efficient and so powerful, and our parent company now sells similar technology in F-Series trucks, that the American public is now getting more interested – especially in the coastal states where congestion is now a problem ...'

The 40th anniversary of the Transit sales will be reached in October 2005, by which time total global sales are expected to be well over 5 million. Outside of North America, no other commercial vehicle could even approach that figure – and by the way, that the brand was still expanding, it looked truly invulnerable.

A solid-looking Transit twin-cab breakdown/ recovery truck, with rear-wheel-drive and twin rear wheels to ensure traction in most adverse weather conditions.

7 Racers

It wasn't only struggling pop groups who slept in their Transits. Many motorsport people did the same: still do, they say. Ever since the Transit came on the scene, it has been vital to any motorsport team, if not to tow the race car or motorcycle, it carries all the spares; if not for conversion into a hospitality unit, then as a temporary home for the entire team.

A Transit has never actually competed in motorsport – not seriously, anyway, but there was one famous occasion, at the Rally of Portugal in 1979, where the organisers arranged a slalom test for all the 'works' service vans to contest. Ford's Boreham-based team had a fleet of Transit vans, usually loaded to the gunwales with mechanics, wheels and spare parts. Chief mechanic, the legendary Mick Jones, was persuaded to take part in the competition and although he did not win, the Transit stayed in one piece. As Mick later commented: 'I was talked into it. I know I could never be a rally driver – and now I know I couldn't win driving tests in a Transit van either!'

Years earlier than this, however, a much faster and much more purposeful Transit 'racer' had been built, the first of a whole series of machines which have beguiled Transit followers ever since. Mind you, in some cases the Transit 'heritage' was lost almost completely.

On all but the most recent project machine, the engines were full-race V8s, mounted behind the cabin, and in every case they had been built for fun, to lighten up the Transit's image, and to give enthusiasts something to talk about.

It all started in the 1970s, and in the next 25 years three different Supervan versions of Ford's most famous van were developed, to amuse the crowds at racing circuits, drag strips and Ford one-make club events. Then, in the 2000s, Ford repeated the trick – twice – once by producing a smart Martini-liveried Transit, and next an amazingly fast and practical 'super-Connect'.

Supervan 1

The first type appeared in 1971 – originally at the Thruxton motor racing circuit at the Easter Monday meeting. Outwardly, this was a conventionally modified Transit van, with an 18cwt payload, although it had flared wheel arches (Escort rally car style) and fatter tyres. The fat wheels and the extrovert character made their own point, for under the skin this was a very hot property indeed.

Ford, which was making good money at the time, and wanted to boost its high-spirited motorsport image even further, elected to produce a mad version of the Transit. The design job went to Terry Drury Racing of Rainham (who knew all about the running gear which was due to go into the new machine). The result was hilarious, and was immediately dubbed 'Supervan'. It only became Supervan 1 by default, when the next-generation type appeared in the mid-1980s.

Instead of a standard structure, Supervan 1 was based round a multi-tube chassis frame of racing type. The modified steel Transit shell was bolted to it at six points, and no thought was given to refinement, or to commercial convenience.

No-one troubled to make drawings, for it seems that the frame design was worked out in the traditional cut-and-shut manner. Components were laid out on Drury's workshop floor, and chalk marks were added around them – maybe Colin Chapman's Lotus company would have scorned this approach, but the early mid-engined Coopers certainly evolved in this manner.

If you opened up the bonnet of Supervan 1, you found it empty – for the engine was tucked away behind the seat. Occupying a large space ahead of the rear wheels was a mid-mounted fully race-tuned 5.0-litre V8 engine (complete with Gurney-Weslake cylinder heads), and a combined ZF five-speed gearbox and final drive transaxle, both of which had been lifted out of a Ford GT40 racing sports car. The rear wheel boxes had to be modified to make space for the vast racing tyres.

This engine was so bulky that the entire top end, the carburettors and the complex exhaust system stuck out through the load-floor pressings of the van. Naturally, there was never any intention to carry anything in this device except for one (or occasionally two) impressed front-seat occupants! Suspension was all-independent – at the front there were some Jaguar XJ6 components, and at the rear some parts of a Cooper F1 car were adapted – along with non-assisted GT40 rack-and-pinion steering, Can-Am racing-size disc brakes at all four wheels, and Firestone racing rubber all added their contribution. Specially cast Revolution alloy wheels of 15in diameter and with 15in wide rims – all helped to make this into a truly crazy piece of design.

With a bellowing 435bhp – no silencing, naturally – this monstrous machine caught attention wherever it went – and that was usually very quickly indeed! Testers on *Autocar*, normally more used to assessing sports cars, or luxury saloons, were quite shattered by the experience. Even using a self-imposed 7,000rpm limit, they recorded an official 0–100mph sprint in 21.6 seconds. Although they never approached top speed at Ford Motorsport's Boreham airfield, where the performance figures were taken, they duly noted that 102mph was achieved in second gear, and that 134mph should have been possible in third – with two more gears still to go! The overall gearing, in other words, was really meant for the GT40 from which the transmission had been lifted, and was a lot too high.

The handling could best be described as extrovert, for although there was plenty of

Supervan 1 was a ferociously uncouth Transit-based machine, with its engine behind the seats (no chance of carrying any goods then!), with fat Firestone racing tyres, and a tendency to lift its front wheels when cornered hard. Great fun.

The original mid-engined Supervan 1 appeared at Brands Hatch on Easter Monday in 1971. Powered by a 5-litre GT40 V8 engine, it could reach 150mph.

We've heard of taking a quick break, but in Supervan 2 this would be ridiculous.

transmission – the vehicle was eventually scrapped and no trace now remains.

Supervan 2

Although everyone had enjoyed the idea of a super-crazy van bellowing around the circuits (no-one ever ignored Supervan 1 when it was out and about), Ford didn't commit to updating the original, so after it was scrapped it was thought there might never be a successor.

Perhaps this was because Stuart Turner had moved on from Motorsport at the end of 1975, and because his successors did not have the same quirky sense of humour. The Transit, for sure, never needed that sort of high-profile exposure.

However, it was no coincidence that when Stuart Turner returned to run Ford Motorsport in 1983, a new device called Supervan 2 appeared just over a year later, in May 1984.

Except for the idea – the same, crazy, for-the-hell-of-it idea – there was no technical connection with the original van. Although Supervan 2 had a front-end style similar to that of the contemporary Transit production machine, behind that nose it was totally different. This time there had been no chalk-marks-on-the-floor type of chassis engineering, for the running gear of the new type was seen to be based on that of the Ford C100 racing sports car – a project which Turner had cancelled so brutally, and abruptly, in March 1983! At least all the

mechanical grip, no attempt had been made to balance the roadholding. At lower speeds it understeered considerably, but when driven by a brave racing driver it usually cornered with the inside front wheel inches into the air.

Demonstrated all round the nation in 1971 and beyond, this machine impressed everyone who saw it. Amazingly, the novelty wore off after a year or so, and Supervan 1 then went back into storage. With demand for genuine GT40 components on the increase – particularly for the ZF

parts were available, for Motorsport had no further use for them.

Supervan 2, in fact, was a much more ambitious design than the original. This time it had been engineered by ace-race-car designer Tony Southgate, who had done so much of the work on the C100 in the early 1980s, and construction was by courtesy of Auto Racing Technology, in which Southgate and John Thompson were partners.

Supervan 2 featured an advanced alloy and carbon-fibre monocoque structure, derived from the C100, and the mid-mounted engine was a modern Ford-Cosworth DFL V8 'endurance' 3.9-litre unit, which developed 590bhp at 9,250rpm. Although it was closely related to the legendary DFV F1 engine, it had been redeveloped to last for many hours of hard endurance running.

The body shell may have looked remarkably like that of a standard, but rather low-riding, Transit shell (and featured all the correct planes, panel positions and proportions), but it was smaller and built from aluminium sheet and glassfibre.

Supervan 2 was the second of Ford's crazy, just-for-fun, high-speed Transits. Built in 1984, and based on the mid-engined Ford C100 racing sports car chassis, it featured an F1-based Cosworth DFL V8 racing engine. It was timed at 174mph on the Silverstone GP circuit.

Supervan 2's colour scheme was in line with the latest from Ford Motorsport. The engine, mounted behind the seats and under the floor, was a monstrously powerful Cosworth DFL of 3.9 litres.

Supervan 2 looked rather like a Transit, but was totally different under the skin. Those ground-effect aerodynamic aids were serious, and the massive scoops in the flanks fed the engine cooling radiators.

included rectangular air intakes to help cool the front brakes, and huge air intakes (almost NACA-style) along the flanks which channelled air into the cooling radiators for the engine. The wheelarch flares were more subtle than in Supervan 1, as were the centre-nut 16in BBS racing wheels, which carried 11.5in wide Goodyears up front, with 14.0in at the rear.

As before, this Supervan was for demonstration and 'fun' purposes only. Tyrrell F1 driver Martin Brundle (these days better known as ITV's F1 pundit, and as David Coulthard's manager), who was thoroughly used to DFV/DFY engine characteristics, was persuaded to grapple with it. After the first-ever test runs at Silverstone, the indomitable Brundle apparently came back to the pits looking pensive.

Although Brundle immediately posted a Silverstone lap in 1min 38sec (which would have been good enough to get him at the front of the grid of a contemporary saloon car race), he discovered that Supervan 2 was actually lifting an inside rear wheel at the chicane, which made things very exciting. Maybe the nose down attitude was too much, and maybe there was too much front grip – other drivers certainly found this to be

Carbon-fibre reinforcement added stiffness, and there was also much tubular stiffening inside the 'loading area'. Not only that, but a pair of genuine 'ground effect' venturi tunnels made up the floor on each side of the Hewland transmission, which explains the cutaway style of the back end.

This time there was no mistaking the 'race-car' intent of this Transit, for there was a massive front under-bumper spoiler, which

Supervan 2 had genuine underbody aerodynamic tunnels which provided positive downforce at high speeds – the outlets to these tunnels explains the lack of bodywork under the rear door. The massive wing above the rear door also helped keep this projectile on the ground.

so. Not even the fitment of a huge transverse rear spoiler at the tail of the roof panel could sort it out completely.

The recorded top speed on the Hangar Straight was 176mph and in addition, the new van was so powerful that it was difficult to keep it straight when blasting away from a halt – pictures apparently existing of Supervan 2 laying rubber for at least the first 20 yards of a drag-strip quarter-mile timed in no more than 12.1 seconds.

Racing driver Chris Craft once chauffeured Marcus Pye of *Autosport* around the Donington Park racing circuit, where he found how easy it was to set the big van into a full-blooded drift around the sweeping corners. Not something for the faint-hearted. Even so, Marcus reminded his readers that: 'Ford have made the best part of two million Transits in the past 20 years. All but two have been called upon to perform mundane tasks and, by and large, they have responded magnificently. Supervan 2 will never pound the motorways, but has already become a crowd favourite at the British Grand Prix. And that's PR!'

Like the original, this was another wonderful, but totally mad idea, that was soon stored away. Although Cosworth reclaimed its DFL engine (which eventually powered some unsuspecting customer's racing sports car), the rest of the machine was thought valuable enough to keep, so perhaps one day …

Supervan 3

The third and final version (so far, at least, but who knows what might happen in the future?) appeared in 1995, when a much-modified version of Supervan 2 reappeared, having been transformed into Supervan 3. The changes were so complete, and the style so much changed, that few realised that this was a conversion, not new build. The most notable feature was the latest-look body shell, complete with droop-snoot and smiley-face grille/front aperture. Door profiles were of the latest type and the front wheelarch flares seemed to fit even more closely to the Goodyear racing tyres.

The chosen colour scheme was more extreme than ever. The simple striping of Supervan 2 had disappeared in favour of a dramatic new white/two-tone blue treatment. Cosworth's name featured strongly on the front spoiler, Ford's sponsors were stacked up on the flanks, and all-in-all this van looked incredibly purposeful.

Supervan 3 was a much-redeveloped version of Supervan 2, with the same rolling chassis, but this time using a Cosworth HB V8 3.5-litre F1 engine, which developed 650bhp at 12,000rpm. The top speed of this Transit was estimated at 200mph.

Under its sleek new skin, Supervan 3 used the same chassis as Supervan 2, but featured essentially the same smiley-face as any other VE83 Transit. Maybe the glass and the general profile was like that of the VE83, but not much more …

Supervan 3 was a seriously efficient piece of high-speed engineering, complete with underbody aerodynamic tunnels to generate downforce, a massive front spoiler/ splitter, and a rear-roof spoiler which really worked. With 650bhp to tame, all that was needed.

Although Supervan 3 was structurally just as before – and it still featured those enormous air-scoops in the flanks to feed the cooling radiators – this time it was powered by a recent-specification 3.5-litre Ford-Cosworth HB F1 V8 engine. This light and compact V8 produced well over 650bhp at more than 13,000rpm, and was of the type which Michael Schumacher and Ayrton Senna had used to win so many races in 1993!

Those were still the days when a Cosworth F1 engine could be matched to less-likely cars than single-seaters, for it was

not only super-efficient, but was still very flexible. The HB, after all, had already been used by the Jaguar XJR14 to win the World Sports Car Championship in 1991.

As before, this was a 'just for fun' projectile, which World Touring Car Champion Paul Radisich (who usually raced Ford Mondeos!) demonstrated on several occasions in 1996.

Would there ever be a successor? It did not look like it, for a later-generation 17,000/18,000rpm V10 F1 engine would never have taken kindly to such treatment, so no further development of Supervan 3 was ever demonstrated. Before long, the Cosworth V10 F1 engine was returned to the makers, and a normal Scorpio 24-valve V6 engine was substituted instead but the van itself then went into hibernation.

Supervan 3, however, was not entirely abandoned, and early in 2004 it was taken out of store, to be rejuvenated. Not only did it receive a smart new paint job, but one of Cosworth's 300bhp 'Supersport' versions of the 24-valve/2.9-litre Scorpio V6 engine was fitted. With 300bhp in place of 650bhp it was maybe not as exciting – but still a lot more powerful than any Transit you ever saw working for its living in the high street!

The Cosworth-Ford HB V8 F1 engine was first seen in 1989, and went on to be a very successful power unit in Formula 1 cars like Michael Schumacher's Benettons and Ayrton Senna's McLarens. This was the 650bhp engine which powered Supervan 3.

No, of course Supervan 3 wasn't meant to be practical, and it was certainly never intended to carry a payload – not even two regular passengers. With a near-200mph top speed, though, it was mighty impressive and gave the Transit brand a real boost.

Transit WRT

When the new-generation Transit was launched in 2000, however, Ford decided that they could, indeed find time for a bit of fun, although maybe not in quite such an extreme way. By this time Ford's 'works'

Compared with the earlier Supervans, the Transit WRT (World Rally Transit) was a totally practical tune up of the rear-drive V184 model. Built in 2000, and used as a promotional tool by the M-Sport team whose Martini-liveried Focus WRCs won so many World Championship rallies, Transit WRT used the standard 2.4-litre turbo-diesel engine which had been tweaked up to 165bhp. The OZ alloy wheels were of rally-type stock. The livery was exactly the same as that used on the Focus rally cars, and the big number 5 on the doors was the permanent competition number used on Colin McRae's cars in 2000.

rally cars – the phenomenal Martini-liveried Focus WRCs in which Colin McRae had so much success – were being run by the M-Sport team in Cumbria.

Although M-Sport's support vehicles tended to be big trucks, there was the occasional need for a Transit van to be used, but these were not as essential to the operation as they had been at the height of Boreham's activities in the 1970s and 1980s.

Even so, in 2000 Ford decided to build up a rather special new-generation Transit,

Where do you put the sarnies, mobile phone and copy of the Sun newspaper then? This was the driving compartment of the Transit WRT of 2000, complete with a sturdy roll cage, Sparco rally seats, full-harness seat belts, and a rally steering wheel, along with extra controls and instruments. Great fun and totally practical to drive.

Crazy? Maybe; practical – but of course! The one-off Connect X-Press was just a good excuse for engineers at Ford's Lommel Proving Ground in Belgium, to have fun. Hidden away is the 212bhp turbocharged 2-litre engine of a Focus RS hatchback, along with many Focus RS chassis components including four-wheel disc brakes, 18in wheels, plus Sparco/Focus RS seats and a full safety roll cage. Speedy delivery, anyone?

What a mixture! The Connect X-Press retained its simple beam rear axle, but with Focus RS rear discs, and more purposeful Sachs dampers.

to give the van's image a further boost. Although it was never called a 'Supervan', and carried the name of Transit WRT (World Rally Transit), it was still an extrovert of machine. As ever, no-one could really spell out a sensible reason for making it, but the Transit WRT, which was built up in a joint effort between M-Sport, and Ford's Press garage in south-west London, combined high performance with great flair. It was a great publicity coup. Ford's rally team had the burgeoning Focus WRT programme to shout about, and there was no better place to replicate the flamboyant Martini livery than on a big van! They knew, and all the anoraks among us knew that they knew, that every decal and every detail had to be right, or someone was bound to complain. Even so, it passes the test – every test. Not only did it look the part but, at a pinch, it could even have worked for its living with Ford's M-Sport team. Relatively speaking it was much more standard than any of the Supervans had ever been – the engine was in the right place, for goodness sake! – but with a claimed top speed of 130mph it could keep up with the latest Focus road cars on most main roads. But 130mph from an engine tweaked by

only 45bhp from standard? Well – we'll believe it, this time …

Transit WRT was based on a standard high-roof 138in turbo-diesel model, with a front-mounted engine and rear drive. However, although the 2.4-litre engine had

been tweaked to 165bhp, there were 8in wide 18in rally-type alloy wheels, and the very Focus WRC-style cabin featured snugly-moulded Sparco rally seats, and a small padded-rim sports steering wheel. The whole van was lowered, springs and dampers had been uprated, and there was a deep front spoiler to make it look mean.

Fully road legal of course – (none of the Supervans ever went close to a public highway, not officially at least) – but they were not for the modest. And why the number '5' on the doors? That was the permanent competition number carried by Colin McRae's Focus WRC in the 2000 season.

And whatever happened to it? At the last count, it was still under Paul Wilson's

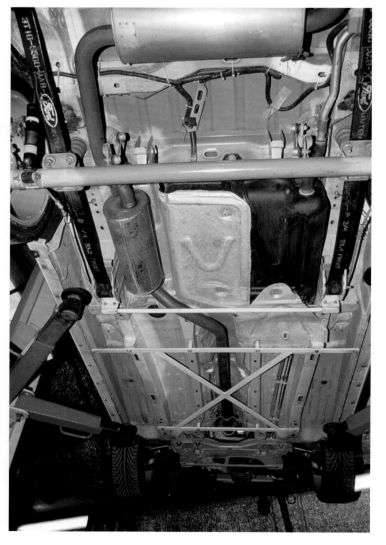

control, and still in great demand. Even so, although the Martini contract has been completed, the livery hasn't been changed.

Connect X-Press

You know how it is. One day at the end of 2003, two engineers at the Lommel Proving Ground in Belgium were chatting at the end of a hard day. One of them looked at the rather battered remains of a pre-production Focus RS, which was due to be crushed. Another looked casually at a short-wheelbase/low roof Transit Connect endurance van. Quite suddenly, it seemed, the proverbial light bulb came on over their head: 'Why don't we make a Focus RS/Connect?'

It was one of those silly suggestions that might have died an early death – but this time round it did not. First of all, development engineer Philippe Castro got permission to do the job. Then, operating on a tiny budget (the only serious expense was in having a sturdy roll cage fitted inside the van shell), and working 'out of hours' he and his colleagues built up the world's fastest Connect.

Completed in January 2004, and liveried with the 'X-Press' logos, this 212bhp machine first met its public in March 2004.

It could, of course, have been an awful hotchpotch – but it was not. Two centuries earlier, Dr Johnson might have said of the dog who walked on its back legs: 'It is not done well, but you are surprised to find it done at all ...' Not in this case. Not only was this a startlingly fast little van, but it was totally practical, reasonably silent, refined – and still capable of carrying loads. (Try putting a load into Supervan 3 and see how far you would get ...)

The secret, in fact, was in the way that the Connect had been packaged in the first place. With the Focus platform and architecture already available for inspiration, the Transit Connect's engine bay had always been made roomy enough to accept any of the same wide range of four-cylinder Ford engines. Since the Focus RS engine had been fitted (tightly, but still snugly) into an unmodified Focus shell, no doubt it could be inserted into that of the Connect? And so it could.

Having stripped out the old Focus RS (and, yes, the body shell from that car *was* then crushed), its entire 16-valve twin-cam engine, five-speed transmission, and cooling package was then transferred into the body shell of the Connect. This, by the way, not only included a turbocharger and air/water inter-cooler, but there was a Quaife automatic torque biasing differential, an uprated AP racing-type clutch and a short-throw gearchange mechanism.

In the meantime, the Connect's interior had been stripped out and inside this body shell a new roll-cage was installed, together with the Ford 'Racing Blue' Focus RS-style Sparco racing-type seats, and a Momo steering wheel.

Under the skin, although Castro and his enthusiastic colleagues had not needed to alter the basic layout of the Connect's suspension (a coil spring/MacPherson strut front end, and a beam axle with half-elliptic leaf springs at the rear), they had worked through it, and improved it in detail.

At the front, the struts had been lowered, allied to up-rated springs and damper settings, with revised A-arms (which helped raise the roll centre height) and a 23mm diameter anti-roll bar. At the rear, the ride height had been lowered to match the nose (there was no need to allow for heavy loads to be carried), the leaf springs had been beefed up, and a 22mm anti-roll bar incorporated roller-bearing locating fixings. The steering, power-assisted as expected, was adapted from that of the Focus RS.

To this, the team also used Brembo disc brakes all round (four-pot at the front, two pot at the rear), and a Bosch Mk 25 ABS anti-lock system was added, 18in OZ alloy wheels were fitted, with 8in wide rims and 225/40-18in Michelin Pilot Sport tyres.

When the media was introduced to this mad little machine, the major surprise was that this was such a complete and appealing packaging. Because the X-Press weighed less than a Focus RS, the straight-line acceleration was even more impressive than ever (although there were no claims, 0–60mph in six seconds was probable), even if the larger frontal area meant that the top speed (not measured at that point) could not have been more than 130mph. On acceleration, those of us who had previously driven Focus RS private cars knew that the turbo effect would chime in at about 3,000rpm, and that the close-ratio gearbox would be a real pleasure to use.

The most amazing feature of the one-off X-Press was that it was such a civilised little projectile. I doubt if the interior was any

noisier than it would be if the normal Connect petrol engines were fitted, the seating was as sexily comfortable as expected, there was a CD installation to play with, and air conditioning to keep the driver cool and collected.

Although the ride and handling had been firmed up considerably from normal Connect settings, it was not nearly as stiff as that of the Focus RS car. Even so, when following a Focus RS at speed on a test track, the Connect did not lurch around, but (aided by the Quaife torque-biasing differential) merely dug in and surged around corners as if it had been bred to do that.

Maybe there was no economic case for trying to put a van like that on sale, but almost everyone who tried the X-Press wondered if a Connect with – say – 130bhp or 140bhp, might find a limited market. Sounds like every white van man's dream to me; high-speed deliveries, anyone?

In many ways this Connect X-Press rear suspension is a throwback to the Mk2 Escort rally cars of the 1970s, for the beam axle was located by leaf springs, with a stout anti-roll bar, and rear-wheel disc brakes.

Compared with the normal Connect, the engine bay of the X-Press was stuffed full of turbocharged 2-litre Duratec RS engine, the turbocharger itself, and an intercooler – all of which, basically, had been lifted from a Focus RS 'hot hatchback'.

8 Transit
Connect

Ford's planners don't miss much. With the Transit family, of course, you could say that they don't miss *anything*. With sales passing the four million mark by 2000, and with more than 200,000 following every year, clearly they had already covered just about every corner of that sector – except one.

For year after year, the Transit had been an only child, and this slightly irritated some of the sales force. Although there was almost a Transit for every occasion, there were limits to how small it could be made. Light vans based on the Escort did a great job, for many years, but after the last Escort of all was produced in 2000, this left a sizeable hole in Ford's commercial vehicle product range.

This was until 2002, when Ford sprang a real surprise. After years of building only one dedicated range of vans, they were ready to add a second to the line-up. Although the new design, intended to take over where previous Ford light vans had left off, had no technical connection with 'Big Brother', it was to carry the same proud name. From the autumn, when deliveries were first made, it was to be called the Transit Connect. That was a move of genius – who needed to know much more, after all, if it carried the Transit name?

At first, observers found the arrival of the Connect a little puzzling, as it looked rather like the Focus-based Fusion MPV (which was launched at the same time), but apart from superficial similarity in the style there was really very little to link the two models. Critically, these two new Fords were not based on the same pressed steel platform. Although what the pundits call 'styling cues' were certainly shared – look at the profile of the headlamps to get a feel for this – it was only under the bonnet, where modern engines and transmissions came out of Ford's capacious 'parts bin', that the two vehicles were seen to share anything.

Initially, the Connect was built solely in a brand-new factory which had been opened in Turkey, and there was much history and logical thinking behind this. Chief Programme Engineer Ernur Mutlu, told me a lot about the genesis of this important project – and about the Turkish connection: 'Ford-Otosan is part of the Koc Group, the largest industrial conglomerate in Europe. The senior Mr Koc was the first to start making deals with Ford in the 1920s, by importing Fords and selling them in Turkey.

'In 1959, the company first started building up Fords from CKD kits – mainly trucks and small commercial vehicles at that time. Over the years, various other products were added to the Turkish line-up, local production of components began, and Otosan was the very first Turkish company to introduce locally-assembled passenger cars into the market – the Reliant-based Anadol model. It has dealt only with Ford throughout its life.

'Transit was introduced to the Turkish market soon after it was launched in Europe [actually in 1967], and at first it was a CKD product – in those days we even had to import the girders to construct the assembly shop! Before long we started stamping our own parts, manufacturing seats, and more trim – and carried on. We had to carry on importing engines and transmissions for many years, but eventually got those locally made as well.'

All this, of course, was many years before a 'small Transit' was even considered, and at that time all Ford-badged products were being assembled at a plant in Istanbul itself. That plant, incidentally, was closed down in 2002 and was finally sold off by Ford some two years later.

In the 1970s and '80s, Ford-Otosan built up its own small but amazingly resourceful team of design, development and manufacturing engineers in Turkey, with an emphasis on trucks like the Cargo (which was still being manufactured in Turkey, many years after all European assembly had ceased). In the 1980s and '90s that team even began manufacturing 'own-brand' engines and gearboxes, including a diesel version of the overhead-camshaft T88 petrol-unit which Europeans still call 'Pinto'.

In 1980, when Ernur Mutlu joined the company, Ford-Otosan was already building the Transit, the Cargo and the Anadol. The Anadol was later replaced by the Cortina Mk III, the Escort also arrived, as did the P100 pick-up truck which had originated in South Africa. Ford-Otosan ended up being a dedicated commercial-vehicle operation in the 1990s.

'With all that manufacturing background,' Mutlu told me, 'as well as a product development group who had experience in commercial vehicle applications, and engine engineering, we started doing other design engineering projects with Ford in Europe. When the time came to make a decision about Connect, Ford-Otosan was selected as a partner.

'In its origins, Connect was in a vehicle segment in which Ford was not represented at that time – the segment that we call the ISV, or integrated style van. Before that, vans of this size were always car-derived, like the Escort van. Peugeot, Citroën and Renault had created the ISV sector, and done good business. When we all looked at trends in that corner of the market, car-derived sales all over Europe were going steadily down, and being replaced by ISV vehicles. That marketplace for these vehicles is still growing, and shows no signs of topping out.'

Ford's marketing and product planning sector saw this coming, saw it become

Introduced in 2002, the Transit Connect was the second, smaller, member of this famous family. Much of the front-wheel-drive running gear evolved from that of the Focus.

As with the bigger Transit range, there was also a Tourneo derivative, which meant that the basic design had been adopted for full-time family use, well-trimmed, and with full seating.

When the Transit Connect appeared, Ford made much of its possibilities for what the advertising industry called 'lifestyle' usage.

established, and decided that the time was ripe for Ford to evolve a new ISV of its own, its very first such product. Even so, the move from 'Good Idea' to 'Van on Sale' had to take time, and the new ISV had to wait its turn in what motor industry watchers know as the 'cycle plan' – the world-wide Ford system, which allocates funds for every project in Ford-of-Europe's massive list of projects. Also, of equal importance, no production facility – no factory with assembly line space to spare – was currently available.

Then came the breakthrough. Ford-Otosan, whose Istanbul factory was old, and bursting at the seams, was already looking to build a new assembly plant some distance out of the city. Its commercial vehicle expertise was well-known, it wanted an opportunity to fill such a new plant, and the ISV programme – coded V227 – came along at just the right time.

In 1996/97 the big deal was finally made. With the approval of the Koc Group, Ford-Otosan agreed to fund the brand-new plant and the new programme, the condition being that the money would eventually come back in what might be called a royalty agreement, and that the V227 would be produced only in Turkey at first.

So it was that engineers from Ford-Otosan and from Ford-of-Europe got

together, and set up the V227 programme. It would be five years – just about par for the course in 'lead time' terms – before the brand-new factory at Kocaeli was ready, and before the new small van had been designed, engineered, developed, and put into production. The fact that the Turks suffered a major earthquake which badly damaged the half-built new plant – a new start being needed – didn't help.

As with the V184/V185 Transits (see Chapter 6), project work on the new ISV V227 started at Dearborn in North America (the 'Connect' name came much later – in the last year of the development phase). Design, styling and packaging work was carried out in Dearborn, and clearly there were styling similarities with other Fords (and Ford-owned vehicles) of this era. Even so, there was no attempt to make the V227's structure in any way common with that of another model: all the sales and production projections told the company that it should stand up on its own.

The Transit V184/V185 team had already become established, so V227 settled into buildings close by, and a considerable European enclave evolved. According to Programme Chief Ernur Mutlu, the entire team lived in Dearborn for two years, taking the Connect project from 'good idea' status, to a running fleet of prototypes.

The main part of the engineering team actually arrived in Dearborn in April 1998,

and left in July 2000. The 'pilot build', in Turkey, had actually begun before the Dearborn office was finally closed down and relocated to Dunton in Essex.

'There was still a lot of travelling involved at that time,' Ernur Mutlu recalls, 'because the manufacturing and also the purchasing centres for this project were located at Ford-Otosan in Turkey. It was only the core engineering team which had been located in the States.'

The Connect, in fact, was unique in two important ways. One was that it was based on an all-new, unique, steel 'chassis' platform, a layout which was both dedicated to the commercial sector. (The Escort vans, to be honest, had always too obviously been conversions of family cars.) Initially, it was thought that a new passenger car model, based on that platform might also evolve, but the requirements for such a model were so special that it had to be cancelled.

'Because the Connect has a unique truck-type platform, it has not had to be compromised in any way,' Mutlu commented.

The other was that it was initially only to be assembled in a modern factory at Kocaeli. As with the larger Transit range, not only was there to be a van with a choice of wheelbases, but there was also to be two well-trimmed versions – shorter and longer types – which were decked out for

Like several other vehicles of its type, the Tourneo (Transit) Connect was effectively a high-roof estate car, with bags of space for a family and all their luggage and leisure gear.

From Day One, the Transit Connect was available with two different wheelbases, and a high roof-line feature.

personal use, as five-seater Tourneo Connect – bus-types.

In the early stages, no chassis/cab derivative was put on sale, but with a reinforced platform-cum-chassis frame one such would certainly be feasible, and I understand Ford's planning team has

considered it, maybe for future years.

Even by 2002, when the Connect went on sale, Ford had already spent up to £400 million on this huge new investment programme. Although this was not the first dedicated automotive plant in Turkey (Fiat and Renault both preceded the Kocaeli plant,

and both have tended to concentrate on passenger cars) it was certainly very large, and very ambitious.

Incidentally, when the Kocaeli factory was originally planned, the decision to move Transit assembly out of Genk had not yet been taken. When that massive move was finally agreed, an immediate extension of the Turkish plant had to be commissioned. The plant, set up with a capacity of 100,000 units a year, was immediately uprated and enlarged, and an extension built, so that 200,000 units could be made. Even so, one compromise was that both 'small' (Connect) and full-size Transits had to share the same paint shop, which became the limiting factor on production numbers.

It soon became clear that the newly expanded Kocaeli plant was already going to be running close to its capacity limits – both full-size and Connect-size Transits were extremely popular – and thought was already being given to a further enlargement of this modern plant. Think of almost any Ford plant in Europe, and in the last twenty years or so the same has applied …

Because Transit Connect capacity at Kocaeli was 100,000, and more than 70,000 were made in the first full year, it was a success right away. In its final life, the Escort van was selling well below 30,000 a year.

This 'ghosted' view shows the mechanical layout of the Connect. A transversely mounted engine and front-wheel-drive, along with a simple rear suspension, guaranteed a sizeable load 'cube' with a low-level platform.

The family, lined up in 2002 – right to left: short-wheelbase Connect, long-wheelbase Connect and high-roof Transit. All these types were assembled in one factory, at Kocaeli in Turkey.

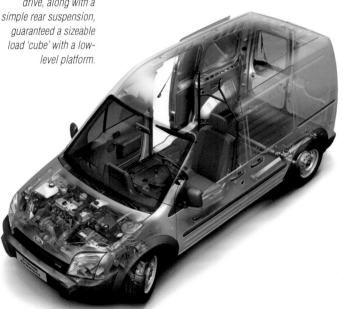

*Mum, dad, the kids and
their leisure gear – all
ready to be loaded into
the Tourneo Connect.*

*On the longer-
wheelbase Tourneo
Connect there was a
very flexible seating
arrangement …*

Accordingly, it was always obvious that the
original Connect was only at the start of a
long and no doubt, comprehensive and wide-
ranging, career. Even in the beginning there
was to be a choice of engines, wheelbases
and specifications. On the evidence of what
always seemed to happen with larger ranges
of Transit, there would eventually be much
more to come.

'It could be considered that way,' Mutlu

agrees, 'it could turn into a number of other
products in the long run. Don't forget,
though, that we immediately announced a
range – engines, wheelbases, body types –
from the start, that no other rival in this
sector has.'

When the Connect was launched, Ford
private-car-watchers immediately realised
that none of the engine/transmission
packages had anything in common with the

... so could anyone complain about lack of stowage room?

full-sized Transits, but were very similar indeed to those of smaller-sized Ford cars, particularly of the much-praised, best-selling, Focus. The 115bhp/1.8-litre Duratec petrol engine was a state-of-the-art 16-valve twin-cam fuel-injected power unit, almost identical to the same engine used in the best-selling Focus and C-Max private cars. Similarly, the 1.75-litre Duratorq turbocharged diesel engines were very similar to those also being used in the early-2000s Focus: the 90bhp derivative, complete with what was known as 'common-rail' fuel injection, was the most economical yet seen in a Transit of any type.

Similarly, the five-speed all-synchromesh manual gearbox, coded MTX75 in Ford-speak, was a heavy-duty version of that found in several other front-wheel-drive Fords – Focus, C-Max and Mondeo among them. There were even some definite similarities with the front-wheel-drive transmission used in the transverse engine/front-wheel-drive version of the 2000s generation Transit.

The MacPherson strut front suspension, too, along with the power-assisted rack-and-pinion steering, were similar in layout to that used in Focus and C-Max models, but almost all the components and their sub-frame had been re-assessed and uprated, to meet the 'truck durability' requirements.

The rear suspension, on the other hand, was simplicity itself, for there was a simple beam linking the wheels, sprung on half-elliptic leaf springs, along with an anti-roll torsion bar. Any more complex type of rear suspension would have involved encroaching into the low floor/wide floor space which was a 'given' factor from the day that package scheming began in the late 1990s.

When welcoming the media to see the

The Tourneo Connect was really a spacious estate car, rather than a converted van.

not only have to provide everything that the long-running range of Escort vans had ever done, but it would also have to meet the challenge which was fast developing from Ford's major rivals.

A new factory

As already pointed out in an earlier reference, by the mid-2000s, built-up Transits of all types would only take shape in two locations. One of these, of course, was to be at Southampton (which still proudly carries the label of 'Home of the Transit' outside its gates), the other being at Kocaeli.

Even before the Connect was engineered, Ford had concluded that it could not be produced at Southampton (which was already bursting at the seams with full-size Transit production), or at Genk (where Transit assembly was due to close down in 2004). In spite of rumours which were washing around the industry at the time, the Connect had never been scheduled to be built at Halewood after Escort assembly closed down.

In the end, the decision was made to expand Ford-Otosan in Turkey, not only so that it became the second centre of full-size Transit assembly, but that it would also be the only location of Connect assembly. Although the Kocaeli plant was initially only one third the size of Genk (where the Transit had always been secondary to the Cortina/Sierra/Mondeo programme), it was already much larger than the Southampton plant, and there was space for further expansion.

Right from the start, Kocaeli had been laid out to assemble Connects, full-size Transits, and even the Cargo trucks which were still an important feature in the Ford-Otosan manufacturing scene. This was a greenfield site, close to the sea, on the Izmit Gulf, south of Istanbul itself. Originally the site had been owned by the Turkish national paper industry, which had trees growing in the era for use as crops in the paper industry. The state concluded that it was not feasible to keep that area for its original purpose and – perhaps amazingly – donated the area to Ford-Otosan.

Initially, thought was given to transferring the Istanbul plant workforce to that area, but it didn't take long before Ford concluded that many more workers would be needed to turn Kocaeli into the European 'Lead Plant'

The Kocaeli factory was brand new in the early 2000s, and became the 'Lead Plant' for Ford assembly of the Transit Connect and full-size Transit models. It was enviably close to the sea, which minimised all the expected transportation problems.

Opposite: Connect assembly under way at Kocaeli. Within two years of launch, more than 1,500 Connects were being produced every week.

new range, Paul Morel, Director, Commercial Vehicles, Ford-of-Europe, pointed out that: 'The new Transit Connect extends Ford Transit's enduring appeal to a new group of commercial vehicle customers in the light and sub-one-tonne medium sector. The Tourneo Connect, on the other hand, has been developed to drive like a car, work like a van and be as tough as a truck – a no-nonsense workmate that also boasts fun family appeal.'

Talking on another occasion, Ernur Mutlu made much of the same features: 'The Connect is the only truck-durability version in this segment. All others, though not car-derived, are still car-based, and therefore not as durable as we have made the Connect. We insisted on that.'

For the new Connect, Ford had several major objectives, which were never going to be easy to meet. The most important one, which was defined by the choice of name, was that this had to be a product which would reflect all the virtues of the Transit, but in a smaller package. Another, quite vital, was that a new corporate van would

engine/transmission assemblies were manufactured in British plants, then shipped out to Turkey.

'Local content built up again immediately after launch,' Mutlu confirmed, 'but we have now reached a satisfactory level. Wherever possible, we sourced components from Turkey, and now there are very few opportunities left over for further localising action.'

By any standards, the Connect was not only completely different from the full-size Transit, but it was also a big step away from the old-type Escort vans. This was inevitable. Escort vans, being based on Escort private cars, had the same basic running gear, and the same limitations on carrying space. An Escort, like the even smaller Fiesta van which slotted in below it, used the same front-end sheet metal, and front-seat passenger seating/control layout, the load carrying 'cube' behind those seats always being compromised by the front-end layout. Even though it was a layout which had worked for half-a-century (before the Escort there had been the Anglia, and before that the Thames van), it was time to move on.

Some of Ford's rivals – notably Peugeot and Citroën in France – had already evolved. These were ISVs, often loosely called 'monocube' layouts, in which body panelling swept upwards from the top of the unique, deep, windscreen, before the roof panel swept back towards the rear, covering a

The Kocaeli plant, being new, allowed lots of space for high-tech assembly of all Transits.

Twin models – the Connect van and the Tourneo Connect mini-MPV, posed artistically with the famous Turkish Bosphorus bridge in the background.

for these vehicles, where volumes would be high. In the end, a core number of Istanbul staff made the move, but the rest of the workforce was hired locally.

To all Ford-watchers, that signalled the serious nature of the Connect programme, and the belief in its long term future. Almost everything, at that stage, was new – a new project, new team, new factory, new location, and a move into a market segment new to Ford.

In the beginning, the whole of the Connect's structure was pressed, assembled and painted at Kocaeli, although the

larger and more useful volume. And there was more. If a unique platform did not have to take account of rear passengers, it could be lower than before and made more robust – yet more opportunity for the payload 'cube' to be enlarged.

When *Autocar* magazine testers got their hands on a long-wheelbase Tourneo Connect (with a 90bhp diesel engine), they were clearly impressed:

'It is considerably bigger in every dimension than Citroën's Berlingo. The wheelbase is 8.75in (222mm) longer than its strong-selling French rival.

'The Tourneo gets hinged doors up front and a single kerb-side sliding door at the rear. The cargo area is accessed through twin vertical doors that kill rearward vision [Ford, in fact, make a virtue of this, on security grounds], but open through 180° to provide a giant loading aperture.

'The 90bhp TDCi we tested may not be as refined as the petrol, but is extremely fuel efficient, with a claimed 43.5mpg on the combined cycle. With a solid amount of low-end shove, the engine is superbly suited to handling big loads and delivers a good turn of speed. The only gearbox available is a five-speed manual.

[Ford's claim for this type was that it could reach 110mph, a quite remarkable pace for what was essentially a commercial vehicle.]

'The Tourneo has car-like precision and remains nicely composed through bends. It copes well with small surface irregularities,

although seriously battered bitumen can send nasty shudders into the cabin.

'But it will be the five-seater Tourneo's brilliant interior packaging and flexibility that will tempt most buyers. The rear bench can be removed in part or completely to boost load capacity to 3,670 litres – much more than its rivals. An optional front seat also folds flat to boost capacity to an enormous 4,360 litres …'

Clearly Ford got it right with the Connect, for it soon began to pick up media awards all round Europe. Before the end of its first season, it lifted not one, but three, awards in the *What Van* annual listings and then, to crown an amazing year, it won the European International Van of the Year contest by a record-breaking margin.

Demand for the Connect built up very rapidly in 2003 – more than 71,000 were built in that year – and the 100,000th Connect was produced in the first weeks of 2004, which was almost as many as the Kocaeli plant could cope with. The good news for the planners was that it immediately hit all its targets, and carved out a successful market share. However, as full-size Transit assembly was closed down in Belgium, and progressively moved to Turkey, there were times when the Connect had to take a back seat to 'Big Brother'. Even so, if the Connect has the sort of career already enjoyed by 'full-size' Transits, every production achievement will rapidly be made obsolete by the next.

What chance *another* 40-year career on the way for *another* Transit?

The Tourneo Connect, with the Istanbul skyline in the background, thus emphasising the Turkish origins of this new-in-2002 Transit model.

Production figures

Site	Year 1965 ,000	1966 ,000	1967 ,000	1968 ,000	1969 ,000	1970 ,000	1971 ,000	1972 ,000	1973 ,000	1974 ,000	1975 ,000	1976 ,000	1977 ,000	1978 ,000	1979 ,000	1980 ,000	1981 ,000	1982 ,000
Langley (UK)	15.3	38.6	34.7	43.0	45.3	45.6	49.7	44.1	1.5	–	–	–	–	–	–	–	–	–
Southampton (UK)	–	–	–	–	–	–	–	11.1	47.2	45.3	43.0	52.6	54.8	37.7	56.4	55.0	37.7	44.6
Genk (Belgium)	32.5	42.6	36.0	27.5	39.3	39.3	36.5	37.0	51.4	43.8	39.8	41.6	50.3	38.8	57.4	51.0	45.9	46.1
Turkey	–	–	0.3	0.9	1.1	1.1	1.5	2.5	3.5	3.8	5.1	5.8	6.1	3.3	4.4	2.4	1.4	3.1
Turkey (Connect only)	–	–	–	–	–	–	–	–	–	–	–	–	–	–	–	–	–	–
Amsterdam (Holland)	–	–	–	–	–	–	–	–	–	–	–	–	–	6.3	11.3	9.4	5.8	–
Australia	–	–	–	–	–	–	1.48	1.33	1.38	1.81	1.79	1.74	1.75	1.19	1.8	0.84	0.22	–
Azambuja (Portugal)	–	–	–	–	–	–	–	–	–	–	–	–	–	–	–	–	8.6	7.6
Belarus	–	–	–	–	–	–	–	–	–	–	–	–	–	–	–	–	–	–
China	–	–	–	–	–	–	–	–	–	–	–	–	–	–	–	–	–	–
Ghana	–	–	–	–	–	–	0.13	–	0.055	0.045	0.035	–	–	–	–	–	–	–
Ireland (Southern)	–	–	–	–	–	–	0.65	0.62	0.475	–	–	–	–	–	–	–	–	–
Israel	–	–	–	–	–	–	–	0.135	0.58	–	0.54	0.7	0.86	0.79	1.65	–	1.2	1.05
Malaysia	–	–	–	–	–	–	0.395	0.335	0.055	1.195	0.96	0.935	1.48	0.04	0.38	0.26	–	–
New Zealand	–	–	–	–	–	–	0.81	0.59	0.4	0.45	0.83	0.62	0.633	0.68	0.84	0.58	–	–
Pakistan	–	–	–	–	–	–	0.11	0.8	1.65	2.39	0.81	1.15	1.19	–	0.98	–	1.2	–
Philippines	–	–	–	–	–	–	0.26	0.18	0.17	0.02	0.09	–	–	–	–	–	–	–
Plonsk (Poland)	–	–	–	–	–	–	–	–	–	–	–	–	–	–	–	–	–	–
Senegal	–	–	–	–	–	–	–	–	–	–	–	–	0.13	0.15	–	0.061	–	–
Singapore	–	–	–	–	–	–	0.135	0.075	0.185	0.105	0.175	0.09	0.185	0.1	0.18	–	–	–
South Africa	–	–	–	–	–	–	0.53	0.42	0.12	–	–	–	–	–	–	–	–	–
Thailand	–	–	–	–	–	–	0.15	0.06	0.23	0.25	0.08	–	–	–	–	–	–	–
Trinidad	–	–	–	–	–	–	0.065	0.09	0.095	0.12	0.105	0.185	0.175	0.243	0.18	0.06	0.04	0.02
Vietnam	–	–	–	–	–	–	–	–	–	–	–	–	–	–	–	–	–	–

The Transit plant in transition in the 1970s. Thirty years on, there has been more development, although not upwards, so that it does not cause any problems with aircraft approaching the single runway.

	1983 ,000	1984 ,000	1985 ,000	1986 ,000	1987 ,000	1988 ,000	1989 ,000	1990 ,000	1991 ,000	1992 ,000	1993 ,000	1994 ,000	1995 ,000	1996 ,000	1997 ,000	1998 ,000	1999 ,000	2000 ,000	2001 ,000	2002 ,000	2003 ,000
	–	–	–	–	–	–	–	–	–	–	–	–	–	–	–	–	–	–	–	–	–
	47.3	42.2	38.9	45.9	60.1	70.7	78.5	69.2	54.5	56.0	58.6	66.3	70.5	68.3	73.4	77.0	66.8	64.5	60.3	54.8	54.3
	34.5	39.1	37.2	60.1	57.9	73.1	84.2	73.4	84.5	75.1	56.8	70.0	82.2	68.3	74.9	85.2	74.5	90.7	100.6	94.4	87.5
	4.2	5.8	5.7	5.5	5.4	4.6	4.7	5.6	6.7	8.2	9.8	4.5	9.6	15.8	25.7	28.3	25.7	36.3	18.2	21.5	39.8
	–	–	–	–	–	–	–	–	–	–	–	–	–	–	–	–	–	–	–	22.2	71.6
	–	–	–	–	–	–	–	–	–	–	–	–	–	–	–	–	–	–	–	–	–
	–	–	–	–	–	–	–	–	–	–	–	–	–	–	–	–	–	–	–	–	–
	3.7	1.2	1.7	2.3	5.1	6.7	10.4	10.9	7.7	4.6	6.5	8.8	9.0	7.4	9.9	10.7	8.1	1.9	–	–	–
	–	–	–	–	–	–	–	–	–	–	–	–	–	–	0.28	0.72	0.12	0.3	–	–	–
	–	–	–	–	–	–	–	–	–	–	–	–	–	–	2.22	2.56	5.1	7.02	7.5	8.966	11.092
	–	–	–	–	–	–	–	–	–	–	–	–	–	–	–	–	–	–	–	–	–
	–	–	–	–	–	–	–	–	–	–	–	–	–	–	–	–	–	–	–	–	–
	2.05	–	–	–	–	–	–	–	–	–	–	–	–	–	–	–	–	–	–	–	–
	–	–	–	–	–	–	–	–	–	–	–	–	–	0.582	1.32	0.08	0.26	0.24	–	–	–
	–	–	–	–	–	–	–	–	–	–	–	–	–	–	–	–	–	–	–	–	–
	–	–	–	–	–	–	–	–	–	–	–	–	–	–	–	–	–	–	–	–	–
	–	–	–	–	–	–	–	–	–	–	–	–	0.1	2.1	2.8	2.0	2.4	0.8	–	–	–
	–	–	–	–	–	–	–	–	–	–	–	–	–	–	–	–	–	–	–	–	–
	–	–	–	–	–	–	–	–	–	–	–	–	–	–	–	–	–	–	–	–	–
	–	–	–	–	–	–	–	–	–	–	–	–	–	–	–	–	–	–	–	–	–
	–	–	–	–	–	–	–	–	–	–	–	–	–	–	–	–	–	–	–	–	–
	0.12	–	–	–	–	–	–	–	–	–	–	–	–	–	0.26	0.22	0.32	0.34	–	–	–

Specifications

Original Transit (1965–1978)

[Ford Project Codes: LCX (short wheelbase) and LCY (longer wheelbase)]

Layout: Integral (unit) construction – van, bus and combi types. Ladder frame – chassis/cab, chassis/cowl, chassis/screen types, and special bodies.

Chassis: Beam front axle, beam rear axle, half-elliptic leaf springs. Recirculating ball steering.

Wheelbases: 106.0in (2,692mm), or 118.0in (2,997mm)

Engines:

Petrol:

1,593cc, ohc, 4-cylinder, 65bhp
1,663cc, ohv, V4-cylinder, 63bhp
1,993cc, ohc, 4-cylinder, 58bhp, or 75bhp or 78bhp
1,996cc, ohv, V4-cylinder, 75bhp
2,994cc, ohv, V6-cylinder, 128bhp

Diesel:

1,759cc Perkins 4/99, ohv, 4-cylinder, 41bhp
1,759cc Perkins 4/108, ohv, 4-cylinder, 49bhp
2,360cc, ohv, 4-cylinder, 54bhp, or 62bhp

Transmissions: 4-speed manual, or 3-speed automatic.

Dimensions: Length, from 192.3in (4,885mm). Payload from 1,345lb (610kg)

Facelift Transit (1978–1986)

[Ford Project Codes: LCX/LCY – known as '1978½ model']

Layout: Integral (unit) construction – van, bus and combi types. Ladder frame – chassis/cab, chassis/cowl, chassis/screen types, and special bodies.

Chassis: Beam front axle, beam rear axle, half-elliptic leaf springs. Recirculating ball steering.

Wheelbases: 106.0in (2,690mm), or 118.0in (3,000mm)

Engines:

Petrol:

1,593cc, ohc, 4-cylinder, 65bhp
1,993cc, ohc, 4-cylinder, 58bhp, or 75bhp or 78bhp
1,996cc, ohv, V4-cylinder, 75bhp
2,994cc, ohv, V6-cylinder, 138bhp

Diesel:

2,360cc, ohv, 4-cylinder, 62bhp
2,496cc, ohv, 4-cylinder, 68bhp

Transmissions: 4-speed manual, or 4-speed + overdrive, or 3-speed automatic.

Dimensions: Length, from 196.7in (4,997mm). Payload from 1,345lb (610kg)

Second-generation Transit (1986–1994)

[Ford Project Code: VE6, and from 1991 VE64]

Layout: Integral (unit) construction – van, bus and combi types. Ladder frame – chassis/cab, chassis/cowl, chassis/screen types, and special bodies.

Chassis: Independent MacPherson strut front suspension, coil springs (SWB from 1986, LWB from 1991) or beam front axle and half-elliptic leaf springs (LWB, 1986 to 1991 only), beam rear axle, half-elliptic leaf springs. Rack-and-pinion steering with independent front suspension, recirculating ball with beam front suspension.

Wheelbases: (1986–1991) 110.8in (2,815mm), or 118.9in (3,020mm). (1991–1994) 111.6in (2,835mm), or 140.6in (3,570mm)

Engines:

Petrol:

1,593cc, ohc, 4-cylinder, 65bhp

1,993cc, ohc, 4-cylinder, 58bhp, or 75bhp or 78bhp, or 87bhp or 96bhp

2933cc, ohv, V6-cylinder (Ford-Germany), 150bhp

2,994cc, ohv, V6-cylinder, 138bhp

Diesel:

2,496cc, ohv, 4-cylinder, 68bhp, 70bhp and 80bhp

2,496cc, ohv, 4-cylinder turbo, 100bhp

Transmissions: 4-speed manual, or 5-speed, 4-speed manual + overdrive, or 3-speed (later 4-speed) automatic.

Dimensions: Length, from 182.4in (4,632mm). Payload (1986–1991) from 1,837lb (833kg), (1991–1994) from 1,753lb (795kg)

Modified front-end style (1994–2000)

[Ford Project Code: VE83]

Layout: Integral (unit) construction – van, bus and combi types. Ladder frame – chassis/cab, chassis/cowl, chassis/screen types, and special bodies.

Chassis: Independent MacPherson strut front suspension, coil springs, beam rear axle, half-elliptic leaf springs. Rack-and-pinion steering.

Wheelbases: 111.6in (2,835mm), or 140.6in (3,570mm)

Engines:

Petrol:

1,998cc, 2ohc/8-valve, 4-cylinder, 114bhp

(China-built VE83s also used a Mitsubishi-based 2.0-litre 4-cylinder engine)

Diesel:

2,496cc, ohv, 4-cylinder, 70bhp or 75bhp

2,496cc, ohv, 4-cylinder turbo, 85bhp or 100bhp

(China-built VE83s also used an Isuzu-derived 2.7-litre/4-cylinder diesel of 78, 93 or 116bhp)

Transmissions: 4-speed manual, or 5-speed manual, or 4-speed automatic.

Dimensions: Length, from 182.4in (4,632mm)

Third-generation Transit (introduced in 2000)

[Ford Project Codes: V184 (rear-wheel-drive) and V185 (front-wheel-drive)]

Layout: Integral (unit) construction – van, bus and combi types. Ladder frame – chassis/cab, chassis/cowl, chassis/screen types, and special bodies.

Chassis: Independent MacPherson strut front suspension, coil springs, beam rear axle, half-elliptic leaf springs. Rack-and-pinion steering.

Wheelbases: 115.4in (2,933mm), 130.0in (3,300mm), or 147.6in (3,750mm)

Engines:

Petrol – rear-wheel-drive only:
2,295cc, 2ohc, 4-cylinder, 141bhp (LPG bi-fuel)
2,295cc, 2ohc, 4-cylinder, 145bhp

Diesel – front-wheel-drive:
1,998cc, 2ohc, 4-cylinder, 75bhp
1,998cc, 2ohc, 4-cylinder, 85bhp
1,998cc, 2ohc, 4-cylinder, 100bhp
1,998cc, 2ohc, 4-cylinder, 125bhp

Diesel – rear-wheel-drive:
2,402cc, 2ohc, 4-cylinder, 75bhp
2,402cc, 2ohc, 4-cylinder, 90bhp
2,402cc, 2ohc, 4-cylinder, 115bhp
2,402cc, 2ohc, 4-cylinder, 120bhp
2,402cc, 2ohc, 4-cylinder, 125bhp
2,402cc, 2ohc, 4-cylinder, 137bhp

Transmissions: 5-speed manual; Durashift automatic-change transmission on some rear-wheel-drive models. From 2004, 6-speed manual on 137bhp rear-wheel-drive models.

Dimensions: Length, from 190.3in (4,834mm) (SWB) to 250.9in (6,374mm) (LWB EL 'Jumbo'). Width (over mirrors) 92.9in (2,360mm). Payload (depending on engine/ wheelbase/spec.) from 1,572lb (713kg) to 5,252lb (2,382kg)

Transit Connect (introduced in 2002)

Layout: Integral (unit) construction.

Chassis: Independent MacPherson strut front suspension, by coil springs, beam rear axle, half-elliptic leaf springs. Rack-and-pinion steering, with power assistance.

Wheelbases: 104.9in (2,664mm), or 114.6in (2,912mm)

Engines:

Petrol:
1,796cc, 2ohc, 4-cylinder, 115bhp
Diesel:
1,753cc, ohc, 4-cylinder, 75bhp
1,753cc, ohc, 4-cylinder, 90bhp

Transmissions: 5-speed manual

Dimensions: Length (short wheelbase) 168.4in (4,278mm), (long wheelbase) 178.1in (4,525mm) Payload range, from 1,378lb (625kg) to 1,984lb (900kg)

Index

RS200 69
Scorpio 18, 21, 28, 82, 83, 85, 105,
    121
Sierra 18, 21, 70, 83, 85, 134
Sierra RS Cosworth 65
Taunus private car16, 17, 55
Taunus Type FK and Taunus Transit
    11, 12, 13, 14, 17, 25, 28, 30
Thames 400E 13, 14, 17, 20, 22,
    23, 24, 27, 28, 30, 31, 135
Thames 800E 10
Thames Trader 28
Windstar 95
Zephyr/Zodiac 14, 17, 18, 22, 35, 37
Fourth Protocol 63
Frentzen, Heinz-Harald 76

Gale, Barry 20, 44, 46, 92, 105, 109,
    110, 112
Gardner, Frank 37
General Motors 59
Glyndebourne 35
Grandinett, Dave 94, 95, 96, 101,
    102

Hallsworth, Mike 51, 60, 63, 71, 77,
    82, 90, 93, 94, 96, 99, 101, 103,
    104, 110
Hammes, Mike 71
Hammonds, Rod 74, 75, 76, 89, 90,
    93, 94, 100, 110
Harrier jump jets 87
Harvey, Simon 86, 87
Hawker/Hawker Siddeley aircraft
    company/products 24, 25, 26
Hawtal Whiting 90, 91, 94
Hayes, Walter 10
Heynes, William 92
Hoile, Eric 75, 82, 89
HRH Princess Anne 47

Iacocca, Lee 22
ICI salt mines 77, 78
Isuzu 89
Iveco-Fiat 42, 70, 74, 75

Jacobson, Andy 91
Jaguar (and models) 92, 93, 104,
    112, 115, 121
Jiangling Motor Corporation 89
Jones, Mick 39, 114

KBD Consultancy 74
Koc Group 126, 128
Kuhne, Norbert 88

LDV – see BMC/British Leyland
Longleat safari park 27
Lotus 114
Lutz, Bob 47, 58

MacLeod, Angus 38, 39, 53, 71, 79,
    112
McLaren F1 car 121
McRae, Colin 123, 124
Martin Walter 29
Matthews, Steve 28
McAllister, Ian 84
Mellor, Ron 62
Mercedes-Benz (and models) 56
Mills, Trevor 96
Mitsubishi 89
Mohammed Ali 34
Monza racing circuit 45, 47
Morel, Paul 134
M-Sport 99, 124, 125
Mutlu, Ernur 126, 127, 129, 132,
    134, 136

Nasser, Jac 84, 90
Nevitt, Peter 58, 60, 69, 71, 74

Packwood, John 51, 58, 62, 64
Parry-Jones, Richard 16, 62, 84, 91,
    113
Penthouse 38
Perkins diesel engines 14, 18, 19, 34,
    42, 44
Peugeot (and models) 127, 136
Poole, Brian, and the Tremeloes 35
Portugal, Rally of 39, 114
Preston, Vernon 13, 14, 16, 19, 28
'Puma' (Duratorq) diesel engine 42,
    93, 99, 102, 103, 104, 111
Pye, Marcus 119

RAC 86
Radio Luxembourg 49
Radisich, Paul 121
Ray, Fred 14
Regents Park Zoo 33
Reliant (and models) 126, 127
Renault (and models) 96, 127, 129
Rhodes, Gary 87
Roberts, Dennis 16
Rochford, Nick 90, 95

Sauber-Ford F1 team 76
Scheele, Nick 110
Schumacher, Michael 120, 121
Selman, Alan 14, 21, 60, 65, 69, 70

Senna, Ayrton 120, 121
Shah of Iran 55
Silverstone GP circuit 117, 118
Slade pop group 86, 87
Southgate, Tony 117
Stewart, Jackie 27, 47
Supermarine Spitfire 25, 27, 44
Symonds, Graham 47, 58, 60, 91,
    92, 98

Terry Drury Racing 114
Thompson, John 117
Toy, Sam 56, 57
Tourneo models 86, 99, 128, 129,
    130, 132, 133, 134, 135, 136, 137
Transit models
    'Redcap' ('Common Van', also V-
        Series) 9, 11, 13, 14, 15, 18, 21,
        22, 70
    Original model (LCX/LCY) 9, 15–41,
        140
    1978 ½ model 9, 42–57, 59, 60, 62,
        73, 140
    VE6 ('Triton') 9, 40, 46, 47, 58–73,
        74, 76, 77, 79, 81, 94, 95, 141
    VE64 74–82, 89, 141
    VE83 9, 74–89, 91, 98, 104, 111,
        112, 120, 141
    VE104/VE129 90, 93
    VE160 93, 95, 96, 105
    VE184/VE185 9, 11, 20, 90–113,
        124, 129, 142
    Concept show van 100
    Connect (and V227) 103, 108, 111,
        114, 123–125, 126–137, 142
    Connect X-Press 123–125
    Supervan 1 114–116
    Supervan 2 116–118
    Supervan 3 119–121
    WRT 121–124
Trotman, Sir Alex (later Lord Trotman)
    93, 99
Turner, Stuart 116

Variety Club of Great Britain 34
Vauxhall – see Bedford
VW 15, 58, 96

Ward, Don 14
What Van 137
Wilson, Paul 124
World Summit 85
Worters, Alan 28

'York' diesel project 38, 42–45, 47